PROACTIVE PUPPY CARE

Preventing Puppy Problems

Tonya Wilhelm

PROACTIVE PUPPY CARE

Copyright © 2015 Tonya Wilhelm

Editor Kimberly Morgan

ISBN-13: 978-1505822298

Printed in the United States of America

Dedication and words of thanks.......

This booklet is dedicated to all of the dogs and their families out there who are living through behavioral issues such as extreme fear or reactivity. I too have lived that stressful life, and this booklet is to help protect those puppies from that lifestyle with a proactive "no worries" approach. In puppyhood you are blessed with the opportunity and responsibility to raise your puppy to be confident and happy.

Thank you to Judy Morgan D.V.M, who inspired me and encouraged me to write my first dog training booklet.
Without your mentoring, this would still be on the "to do" list.

A big thank you to my editor Kimberly Morgan, who took my jumbled grammar and sentences and turned them
into a work of art. Without you, this booklet would be hard to follow.

My thanks would not be complete without mentioning my wonderful mother.
Without your kindness, generosity and support I would not be the woman I am today.
Thank you, Mom, from the bottom of my heart.

Contents

Introduction

Congratulations on your new puppy! Adding a puppy to your family can be one of the best joys in life. The pure joy of watching a puppy frolic in the yard chasing something as simple as a leaf is priceless. Oh, and the wonderful smell of puppy breath and kisses are to die for. But puppy raising can be very challenging if you are not equipped with the correct tools or do not realize what is involved.

Puppyhood is the most important time in a dog's life. They are like little sponges soaking up experiences and learning what is safe, appropriate and fun. You will not be able to redo this critical period in your puppy's life, so take advantage of their development and teach them the skills needed to lead a happy life. A good puppy parent will be able to mold their puppy into a confident, safe, happy dog with whom they can spend the next 10-15 years. The work you put into your puppy now will help to ensure a "good dog" in the future. Be prepared for some ups and downs and remember that patience and a good sense of humor are important. If you have that attitude, raising a puppy is truly a blessing.

This booklet is intended to provide you with some basic information on the development of your puppy and how to successfully teach them to live in a human world. This booklet gives a strong focus on the behavioral health of your puppy, and on preventing common and detrimental behavior problems. Prevention is always the best tool. Use it often.

Positive Reinforcement Training Many dog trainers advocate many different training methods. The only method I embrace and always recommend is positive reinforcement. The reason I use this method is simple: **IT WORKS!** Positive dog training is scientifically proven to be effective and enhances the relationship between dog and owner. Dogs that are trained only with positive techniques have fewer behavior problems than those trained with harsh or negative methods. Dogs that are taught using punishment based training are significantly more likely to show fear responses.[1] Positive reinforcement is a tool to reinforce good behavior and eliminate undesirable behavior. This approach builds **self-esteem** and inspires **confidence** in your dog. And it's easy -- once you get the hang of it!

In other words, this means that ***something good is given to the puppy to make a desired behavior stronger.*** This can be treats, praise, access, or toys. Your puppy will repeat behaviors he finds rewarding. Knowing this allows you to choose the behaviors you would like to keep by reinforcing them. By doing this, you are encouraging your dog to repeat the behavior.

Dogs' feelings of esteem are very highly influenced by their interaction and relationship with their owners. All dogs need to feel loved and accepted, and you can communicate those feelings to your dogs by the way you respond to them. Once you develop the habit of consistent positive reinforcement, you'll see that communicating is easier than ever before.

No pain/intimidation=Everything to gain! There is never a good reason to use pain, fear or physiological intimidation with your dog. Dogs are not out to get one over on us, or to dominate the household. Pseudoscience and television programs have played a negative role in real behavioral research. Dominance theory is outdated numerous studies and research have proven it ineffective, and shown that it can cause more harm than good.[2]

1

Although some fear tactics can suppress some behaviors for the short term, the likelihood of them reoccurring in the future is high. This can cause damage to your relationship with your dog, and your puppy's association with what they were being "corrected" for can be detrimental. Your dog may not express that he is uncomfortable in a situation because he was corrected, but that does not change his underlying feelings, and he will then become a ticking time bomb. These are often the dogs that bite "out of the blue" because they were not free to express their feelings (by growling, backing up, etc). Their emotions should have been addressed, not suppressed.

Motivation is the first order of business! **No motivation=no training.** Keeping your puppy's training enjoyable is the best way for your puppy to learn. You want your training to be a fun and engaging experience so that you and your puppy look forward to your lessons.

A good motivator is something your puppy really looks forward to. If you are using a toy as a motivator, *it should not be a toy your puppy has unlimited access to*. If he can get that toy anytime he wishes, why would he work for it? A great food motivator is when you see your puppy's eyes light up when you give him the treat. Something he would do flip-flops to get.

When working with your puppy, you will need a wide range of motivators. You will be teaching your puppy "*expensive behaviors*" and "*inexpensive behaviors*." An inexpensive behavior something relatively easy for your puppy, and you would use a lower-ranked motivator. If you want your puppy to do something difficult, it is an expensive behavior, and you would want something extra-special and exciting.

Work-To-Eat/Work-To-Play Often puppy parents are worried about using food or toys in training, thinking they will only respond if the motivators are present. If used correctly, rewards are like a "paycheck" to the puppy. The idea is for you to make rewards only available in return for good behavior or when counter-conditioning a potential fearful situation. Your puppy needs to learn to work for a living; only then will he be motivated to work for you.

Throughout this booklet, you will see the common phrase *"give him a treat"* during various situations and training exercises. These treats are going to be part of your puppy's daily caloric intake. No dog food bowls are necessary for eating; your puppy will eat his food calories throughout the day for life lessons.

Calories are very important when using food as a reward. Remember your puppy is going to eat his calories during daily training lessons. Toss those kibbles into the pockets of all family members who are interacting with your puppy. If your puppy will work for his kibbles for inexpensive behaviors such as butt on the ground, these make excellent rewards. You can use cooked meats for expensive behaviors such as walking on a leash or coming when called. Calculate the meat calories into his daily calories. Dogs eat meat, so eating these necessary meat calories as whole foods in training can replace a portion of the dry kibble calories. Review the section on *Healthy Food and Proper Weight pg. 40*

Will my puppy always need food for the rest of his life? Well, yes he will always need food to survive. How you choose to use those food calories is up to you. When your puppy has learned a new behavior and developed a good habit, you will be able to fade how often you reward that behavior. However, just like a sport, he should practice any behaviors you want to keep regularly and should be occasionally rewarded for them to keep them strong. Dogs are very intelligent animals and love to be active and learn in a positive environment. Therefore, it is important to keep challenging your dog throughout his life by teaching him new skills, games, behaviors and increasing the difficulty level of a task. When you do this, you are going to be rewarding that new skill set, and once again increasing the bond you have with your dog.

Taking Food and Treats Gently Ouch! Having your fingers chomped on by your puppy as you try to give him a treat is not a pleasant feeling. If you want to save your fingers, here is a training exercise on teaching your puppy how to take food from your hand gently. This is great daily exercise to do in the morning with your puppy's breakfast.

❑ Hold a piece of his kibble between your thumb and index finger and present it to your puppy's mouth area. If your puppy snatches at it and you feel teeth, just hold tight and do not release the kibble. Be careful not to pull your hand back, or move it around. Continue to hold the kibble until you either feel your puppy's lips, or tongue and no teeth, then as soon as you do, allow your puppy to have the kibble. Repeat with the next kibble. You can do this with his entire breakfast, or 20 or so kibbles. **Tip:** Until your puppy has a mastered taking food gently, when you want to give your puppy a treat for a reward and he still is a bit snappy about taking treats, present your puppy with his training reward in an open palm (like when you feed a horse), so he takes the treat nicely. This also is the best way for children to offer treats to puppies.

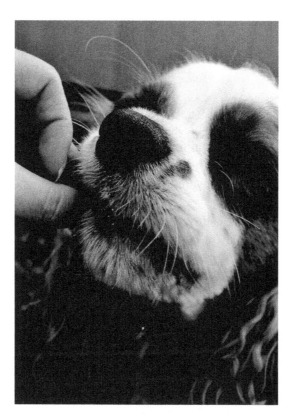

Getting Started

Management Effective puppy training starts with great management. You will want to do whatever you can to prevent a behavior you do not like, or won't like, from happening. This will allow you the opportunity to teach your puppy the behavior you would rather he have. It is a lot easier and more successful to *prevent* a bad habit than *change* one. Plan ahead to set yourself and your puppy up for success. If you have good management in place, it will be next to impossible for your puppy to "misbehave," leaving you plenty of opportunities to reinforce good behavior.

- ❑ **Puppy-proofing** is vital if you want to make certain that your puppy does not eat anything he is not supposed to. If he cannot get access to the remote control, your favorite shoes, or the turkey dinner, he will not be able to eat it. Puppy-proofing your home is the same idea as if you were to bring a baby into the house. You would not allow the baby to reach the stove, so you should make sure your puppy can't either.
- ❑ **Baby gates or shut doors** are a great example of a good management tool. They allow you to keep your puppy out of rooms you don't want him to enter. Or more importantly, keep him from going in them and destroying valuable items. A baby gate at the top of the stairs or start of basement stairs can also save your puppy's life from a potential fall.
- ❑ **Hollow treat toys or safe chew treats** are excellent ways to keep your dog busy when you are unable to entertain him. Puppies are very active and love to chew and gnaw on items. Teaching your puppy about rewarding and appropriate things to chew on is important if you want to save the legs of your table. Review the sections on *Stuffing A Hollow Chew Toy pg 5. and Safe Dog Chews and Bones pg. 45*
- ❑ **Treats and rewards** are your friends during puppy training. Each morning toss a handful of your puppy's kibbles or treats into your pocket. You can then reward your puppy for good behavior no matter where you are. If you have rewards on you at all times, you will not miss any opportunities to let your puppy know he made the right choice. By not going to the "treat jar" for a reward, this also helps teach your puppy that he does not need to see food in order to have a reward. The opportunity is always there, increasing your chances of successful training.
- ❑ **A leash and harness** are excellent management tools in puppy training. When you are busy in your home office and would like your puppy to stay close, you can hook him to a harness and leash and place the handle of the leash under your chair or foot. He can be close to you, and you can easily grab his leash and take him with you if you decide to go in another room, or he needs a potty break and walk. You can also provide one of his stuffed hollow toys or safe chew treat during this time for chewing.
- ❑ **Tethering** is when you take your puppy's leash and wrap it to a sturdy piece of furniture like the sofa or railing by the front door. Ideally these will be extra leashes that are always attached to specific places so you can quickly hook your puppy up when needed. For example, if you have a tether positioned somewhere near the front door, when the door bell rings, you can quickly hook your dog to his tether before opening the door to prevent escape and jumping behavior. Another application is during your dinner time. Instead of having your puppy hovering around your feet, you can tether him up to an appropriate spot nearby while you eat. A good rule would be to provide him with one of his chew options at this time. You should **NEVER** leave your dog unattended while attached to a tether; he could easily wrap himself up and even strangle himself if unsupervised.

- ❑ **Exercise and human play** are important management tools in raising a well-behaved puppy. I consider these two items a package deal because I do not consider running around the yard without a person effective exercise. After all, if you are not there, the management is not in place. Your puppy will pick up all kinds of bad habits without your supervision and direction.
- ❑ **Crates** or kennels are another great management tool during puppyhood. It can provide a safe and puppy-proofed area for your puppy to sleep in while you are away, or not able to keep that constant eye on him. It is also a wonderful way to travel with your puppy to prevent him from moving around the car, and it also helps in motion sickness.

Stuffing A Hollow Chew Toy I love using rubber hollow chew toys to keep puppies and dogs busy and engaged. I recommend this to virtually all my dog training clients. Why? Well, for starters, puppies love to chew. Puppies get bored easily and using food toys is a great canine enrichment activity. There are times in our lives that we need to keep our puppy busy while we engage in another activity. Using a stuffed chew toy can be a great way to keep our energetic puppies busy.

Teaching your puppy how to use a treat toy might take a little trial and error. But do not worry, once your puppy gets the hang of things, a filled treat toy will be a great way to keep him busy. Start with something wet like canned dog food or organic peanut or almond butter and smudge it on the outside of the toy. You want to make it easy enough for your puppy to want to interact with the treat toy. This step may take a few days. You are looking for your puppy to anticipate the chew toy and eagerly lick away. Once this happens, smudge your wet food in the opening of the toy, so he has to start licking inside the toy for his reward.

Once your puppy is readily interacting with his treat toy with food in it or on it, it is time to raise the bar a bit more. If you are home cooking or using high-quality canned dog food, just place a couple of spoons inside your puppy's toy. Then hand over the filled toy to your puppy to figure out this new challenge.

If you are using dry dog food, place about 1/4 to 1/8 cup of the dry food in a bowl and add about 2 spoonfuls of canned dog food. Stir and mix together so that the dry kibbles are coated with the canned dog food. Now place that mixture inside the toy and give the stuffed toy to your puppy to enjoy.

When he has mastered this step, it is time for the real fun to begin! Double your dry kibble and canned food mixture and place 1/2 the mixture inside your puppy's toy. But this time place the toy in the freezer. Once frozen, remove and stuff the remaining mixture on top of the frozen mixture and present to filled toy to your puppy. Your puppy will be able to enjoy the unfrozen treat immediately as the bottom half starts to thaw slowly. The frozen mixture will be quite challenging to master, which will keep your puppy busy longer.

Once mastered, place the entire mixture inside the hollow toy and freeze. This should keep your puppy busy from anywhere between 10 minutes to 35 minutes. Now you can do some other things while your puppy is happily chewing away.

If you are feeding your puppy a home-cooked diet or part of a home-cooked diet, this will allow you to mix up the items stuffed into the toy. By doing this, your puppy will continue to find the filled treat toy interesting and engaging. Have fun, and I'm sure your dog will thank you for it.

Tip: If your puppy leaves the toy and is not interested, it typically means the food inside is not valuable enough, or it is too challenging. Increase the value, and decrease the difficulty. Most of these hollow dog toys are dishwasher safe (top shelf). But I prefer to use cool water and a baby bottle scrubber to clean because I do not like rubber to get hot.

Calorie Tip-Remember, you will be using your puppy's daily calories for training and toy stuffing. So plan accordingly.

Crate Training is a great tool in your management plan. It can also be a wonderful management tool when there is too much household activity to manage your puppy effectively with one of the other management options. Another bonus in crate training is if your puppy ever needs to stay in your veterinarian's office or goes to the dog groomer or boarding facility, he will be comfortable being confined to a crate. Taught correctly, this space can be a very comforting place for your puppy to sleep in. You may even find that your puppy seeks out his crate when he is tired, or needs a getaway. Do allow your dog the privacy he is seeking when he is in his crate.

Crate size is the first thing to consider when choosing a crate for your particular puppy. Depending on the breed of puppy you have, you may need to purchase a smaller crate than the size he will ultimately be using. Your puppy's crate should be large enough that he can stand up, turn around and stretch his legs out. Do not purchase a crate that makes your puppy hold his paws in an uncomfortable position. Remember, you want your puppy to enjoy his space and be comfortable inside his crate. On the flip side, too large a crate might encourage your puppy to eliminate in one corner and sleep in the other. Some crate styles such as the wire crate often come with a divider so you can partition the crate smaller then allow more space and eventually remove it as your puppy grows.

Crate style is the second decision in your purchasing choice. Dog crates come in all kinds of styles and choices. You can purchase wire crates, plastic crates, wood crates, or heavy duty mesh fabric. All the styles have their pros and cons. One thing to consider is that your puppy is still in the chewing stage so a mesh crate might not be the best solution quite yet, and depending on the wood style, this too might be risky. Plastic dog crates have less opportunity for ventilation and do not fold up or store very well. Wire crates are not the best to look at and dogs have been known to push the crate in such a way that the wire sides unclip and collapse. Use zip ties to secure the ends if this is a concern. Personally, I have multiple wire crates and a mesh crate that I take with me to dog events that my dog can use at our display table if he wants to retreat from the crowd.

Crate location is the next decision. I personally feel that having your puppy's crate in your bedroom is the ideal location, and offers several benefits to your puppy. The first benefit is that by allowing your puppy to be in your bedroom at night, you are increasing the ever-important bond with your puppy. Second, you will be able to hear your puppy at night if he needs to go out for a potty break during potty training or if he develops diarrhea. Third, if your puppy ever wakes up in distress from a loud noise such as a thunderstorm you are there to address the situation immediately.

If you choose another location other than your bedroom for your puppy's crate, you will want to think about that particular environment. Remember that your puppy's crate is supposed to be a pleasant and peaceful location. So do not place your puppy's crate in a dingy spot or a noisy spot. Think about what happens during the day and how that will affect your puppy. Is the area noisy? Is there enough light, natural or artificial, to be comforting?. Is there too much light that might be glaring and uncomfortable? All that said, you can have more than one crate in your house. Maybe you have a crate in your bedroom and a second crate in the main part of the house for easy access during quick crating times while you are home.

What to put inside the crate depends on your puppy's chewing habits. Because puppies tend to do a lot of chewing and it can be dangerous and risky to leave bedding inside your puppy's crate for your puppy to chew and swallow, I suggest introducing bedding gradually. The same would apply to leaving a toy or chew toy with your puppy. You will want to ensure first that your puppy can safely interact with his toys before leaving him unattended with one.

Setting the right mood can increase your chances that your puppy will like his crating experience. This topic goes back to your crate location choice. Again, look for a place that is not noisy. I never recommend placing a puppy crate next to a window unless you pull the blinds or shades. The outside world is full activities such as children playing and small animals moving about. If your puppy can view this from the crate it can cause anxiety or even agitation so to promote healthy sleeping habits make sure the view from the crate is limited.

Warmth is important to encourage your puppy to sleep. Make sure the room your puppy is sleeping in is comfortable and not chilly. Once you are confident that your puppy will not chew his bedding, a nice plush dog bed and blankets are perfect for inside your puppy's crate.

Lighting is another piece of the mood puzzle. Darkness is wonderful when you are in the room with your puppy during crating. But the times when your puppy is crated and you are not sleeping in the same room with him, keep the room dim, but not pitch black.

Music is one of my favorite pieces of the crating process. Various research studies such as Dr. Deborah Wells's *The Influence of Auditory Stimulation on the Behaviour of Dogs Housed in a Rescue Shelter*,[3] have shown that classical music helps to soothe dogs. Dr. Susan Wagner took it further with another study, *BioAcoustic Research and Development Canine Research*,[4] and determined the best sequences and notes to use for optimal results for a dog to relax, then created the *Through A Dog's Ear* CD. I highly recommend playing this CD during any crating times and placing the track on repeat. After hearing the CD a few times, your dog will become conditioned to relax and calm when they hear it playing.

Crate Training Exercises

Ideally you should introduce your puppy to his crate gradually and often. Depending on your puppy's past experiences with crates, this can be a slow process or a very quick one. Please judge your puppy's behavior and anxiety carefully and when in doubt seek the advice of a professional. Making your puppy view his crate as a positive and relaxing place to be is important for a lifetime of success.

- ❑ Set your mood with lighting, blinds, music, etc. The goal being that a training exercise should feel like real life, and real life is just a training exercise.
- ❑ Remove your puppy's collar and harness. Dog collars and dog tags can easily get caught on crate wires, wrapped in your puppy's foot, or even caught on his mouth.
- ❑ Start by having some tasty treats and toss them into the crate. When your puppy goes into the crate, tell him what a good dog he is and toss some more inside. When he comes out of the crate, and looks at you for some more, just smile at him. Toss a few more into the crate, and repeat the process.
  - ❖ After a few repetitions, see if starts to stay in his crate longer looking for you to toss more treats into his crate. If he does, start tossing a treat in every 5 seconds, 10 seconds, and gradually increase the duration between treat tosses. If he pops back out of his crate and looks at you, smile again, this time waiting to see if he goes into his

crate on his own. If he does, jackpot that behavior by tossing one treat, two treats, three treats...until you toss in ten quick treats.

- ❑ In your next, session, repeat the above sequence, but this time, when your puppy is inside the crate, softly shut the door, and feed him treats through the slots while calmly telling him how wonderful he is. Open the crate door to let him out, and repeat the sequence, each time increasing the time the door is shut before the treat delivery.
- ❑ Once your puppy is enjoying a few minutes inside his crate with the door shut it is time to continue increasing the real life scenario.
  - ❖ If you have two mobile devices with a video chat application installed, this would be a perfect time to use them. You can place one device pointing at your dog while you hold the other. You will be able to see your puppy's reaction to ensure he is being successful and not stressed. I do not recommend talking to him during this stage because you will not always be able to talk to him during real departures and crate time.
- ❑ After you shut the crate door, turn around and walk four steps away then return to your puppy and toss in a treat. Repeat taking four steps five times. Start to increase the number of steps you take away from your puppy before returning. Continue this process until you reach the bedroom door, step out of the bedroom, then return to your puppy. Repeat this process, increasing the distance and time you leave. Your goal is for your puppy not to be stressed, so take your time and decrease criteria if your puppy seems stressed.
- ❑ Continue to build the length of time you are away from your puppy before calmly returning with a treat. As you build this time to ten minutes or more you may hear a little whimpering. This is normal; do not return to your puppy during this time. *You only want to return when your puppy is quiet.* Your goal is for your puppy to fall asleep during crate times. To speed up this process, the below evening scenarios are recommended.

Your bedtime routine and sleeping arrangements can jump-start your puppy's conditioning to sleeping in his crate. When you are ready to retire to the bedroom, turn a calming CD on such as *Through A Dog's Ear*. Calmly give your puppy some snuggles and affection then toss a treat inside his crate. Once he goes inside, close the door and toss one more treat inside. Tell him good night and get into bed yourself. That is it. If he starts whimpering, do not pay attention to him. After a few days, he will realize this is bed time, and his whimpering will subside. If he does not, and you are practicing the above crate training exercises, please seek a professional for guidance. **Tip:** If your puppy still is whimpering at the beginning of this routine, start earlier so that he finishes whimpering before you really wanted to go to bed.

Additional Considerations
- ❑ Keep the crate door open during the day, and anytime you notice your puppy going into it, tell him how wonderful he is, and toss him a treat. You can also leave treats in the crate for him to find on his own.
- ❑ Crates can be weaned off gradually after your puppy is fully housetrained and trustworthy (1-3 years). However, always leave the crate door open; you may be surprised to see how much your dog loves his peaceful crate.

Letting your puppy out of his crate should be a calm event. Do not get high pitched and overly enthusiastic, or your puppy will get jumpy, vocal and may even submissively pee. Instead, grab a few treats or dog kibbles prior to entering his crate room. Open your puppy's crate calmly and immediately drop a treat on the floor. If your puppy wears a harness and leash to go outside, quietly attach his equipment while giving him a few treats. As you start to walk to the outside door with him, drop a treat of dog kibble on the floor every few steps to encourage your puppy to keep four on the floor when greeting and walking. If you have a fenced-in yard, you can just start to drop a treat or kibble from the start and start the walking and dropping process. Over time, your puppy will have a great habit of calmly leaving his crate and keeping four on the floor while going outside. When you see this habit develop, you can then start to decrease the quantity of treats or kibble until they are faded altogether. Remember, you are setting your puppy up to learn good habits and routines, instead of trying to un-train a bad habit or routine, which is always harder to teach.

A Word Of Caution Please be thoughtful when using your puppy's crate. Dogs left alone too long can suffer from lack of social contact, physical exercise, and mental exercise. Common sense tells us that crating a puppy longer than he comfortably can "hold it" is too long. A good rule of thumb is that your puppy should not spend any longer in hours than he is months old. So if your puppy is three months old, he should not be in his crate longer than three hours at a time. Dogs or puppies that must remain in their crates longer than six hours should have someone come over in-between to have a potty break and social interaction.

Confidence Building

No Worries One of the most important things you can teach your puppy is to not worry. If you would like your puppy to become a great family dog who is not afraid of people, thunderstorms, loud noises, or unusual environments, then now is the time when you have the most influence over your puppy's psyche.

Behavioral problems in dogs usually develop from a lack of confidence. Instead of trying to fix a problem such as fear of fireworks or strangers, work hard on preventing them in the first place. You can take control and implement a proactive approach to your puppy's development. This is where my *No Worries* training program comes into play.

No worries. A pretty simple concept when you think about it and truly not that hard to put into action if you think ahead and think about what your dog is feeling. *Oh yes, they are very emotional creatures and very complex.*

Here are a few ideas to get you started. We will go over some of them in more detail later in this booklet. Prevention, prevention, prevention. Do not wait for a potential problem to happen, have Pavlov on your side. When reading the list, remember the **No Worries** mantra!

- ❑ **Training Methods**-We certainly do not want our dogs to be intimidated, or scared of us in any way! We are supposed to be their teacher, parent and someone they can trust and turn to in times of uncertainty. Positive training methods only!
- ❑ **Thunderstorms**-Remember the No Worries concept and your proactive approach. Clap of thunder=toss of high value treat, such as real meat
- ❑ **Dogs Barking**-When your puppy hears a dog barking=toss a treat
- ❑ **Garbage Truck, Fire Truck, Bicycles, Sirens, Vacuum Cleaners**-Unusual or loud noises=toss of high value treat such as real meat
- ❑ **Strangers, Kids, Men**-A fear of strangers is such a shame and easily avoidable. Humans=food rewards and games

Are you seeing a trend here? Do not wait to see if your puppy is going to have an issue with anything, instead start to work actively on a prevention plan. You are teaching your puppy that good things happen when potentially scary or unusual things are around. This, in turn, helps to teach your puppy not to worry, and in the end, you get a dog who will look up at you when those things are presented to him in his life.

Yes! I do try to have rewards on me at all times, particularly if I'm working with a new puppy, or actively working on changing a behavior. Your puppy is always learning, and if you want to teach and guide him into becoming a well behaved and confident dog, every opportunity is a teachable moment. And if you recall earlier in this booklet, your puppy is using his everyday calories for his training and behavioral lessons. He is in essence getting fed his meals for desired behaviors.

Over time, repetitions, and puppy growth, you will be able to reduce the amount of food and toy rewards used gradually. I want to see a puppy reliably *not reacting* in a situation, and being calm and/or looking at me before I even think about fading the reward system. But I urge you not to do this too soon. By actively reinforcing good behavior and conditioning your puppy that possible scary things are not to be feared, you are creating a coat of armor for your dog. In the future when an unforeseen scary or unusual situation arises, he will be armed with the confidence to allow the situation to roll off his shoulders.

Socialization People with puppies are often told that they must "socialize" their puppies. But what is socializing? Why does everyone say it is so important? And what is good vs. bad socialization experiences and exercises?

Puppy socialization is a process in which you gradually introduce your puppy to a variety of people, places and things in the early stages of their lives. The opportunity for making the best impact on your puppy's socialization is between 3 weeks and 4 months of age and continues until your puppy is about 6 months old. So by the time you bring your puppy into your home a good portion of his socialization window has already passed. However, puppies go through various "fear periods" during the first 18 months of their lives, so do not stop an active socializing program once your puppy is 6 months old. During a puppy's adolescent period (6 months thru 18 months) puppies can have a decline in confidence if they are not continually exposed to new situations in a positive and controlled way.

Why is a good puppy socialization program important? Socialization is critical because it can mean life or death. That may sound drastic, but lack of good socialization during a puppy's first 18 months of life can seriously increase the possibility of behavioral problems later in life. These behavioral problems can include extreme fear and aggression. According to a study conducted by the National Council on Pet Population Study and Policy, behavioral problems, including aggression toward people or nonhuman animals, were the most frequent reasons for a dog's surrender to a shelter.[5] The sad part is that in most cases, appropriate and adequate socialization experiences can prevent these behavior issues from developing in the first place.

Good puppy socialization is the key here. You must actively work on controlling your puppy's interactions to ensure a positive and stress-free experience with what you are trying to socialize him to. If you are introducing him to children and a mob of five-year-olds scream and run toward him, it is unlikely he will have a good experience, and in turn may develop some serious issues around children. It is particularly important to monitor interactions your puppy has to make sure they are enjoyable. *Gradually* expose him to noises and sights at an increasing intensity so you can evaluate how he is feeling. Remember your *No Worries* lessons and reward your puppy around different situations.

Reinforce confident behavior and help him if he is fearful! If your puppy shows any signs of being fearful, or stressed, you must make sure you are addressing his needs and decreasing his fear by allowing him to move away from what he finds scary or intimidating. Try moving your puppy farther away from the "scary" source. Once your puppy is relaxed, reinforce this behavior with a tasty treat or play.

If your puppy has a bad experience with something, try to set up a similar situation in a less stressful way. Be prepared to reward heavily for brave behavior. Start with your puppy from a distance he feels comfortable at while feeding him high-value rewards such as cooked meat. Over various sessions, gradually decrease the distance. *Make sure you are moving at his comfort level; do not do more than he is ready for.*

Daily socializing exercises will increase your chances that your puppy will develop into a confident and behaviorally healthy dog. Taking your puppy on a new little adventure each day will help build his self-esteem and decrease the likelihood that you will be faced with a behavioral problem in the future. If you are not able to go on an adventure one day, set up something new for him in the home to investigate such as a room-full of pots and pans. Allow him to sniff them, walk on them, see his reflection, etc. Be creative in your new home adventure exercises.

Below are a few socializing ideas to get you started.
- ❑ **People-**Adult females, men, senior citizens, teenagers, children, toddlers, infants, people in unusual clothing (uniforms, hats, sunglasses, large or thick jackets), different nationalities, person using a wheelchair, walker, cane, or crutches
- ❑ **Places-**Different parks, playgrounds, veterinary hospitals (for fun visits), dog grooming salon (for fun visits), dog kennel (for fun visit), pet store, dog-friendly stores and shopping plazas, dog shows, different friends' homes, hotel, woods, and beaches
- ❑ **Things-** Bicycles, cars, motorcycles, trains, roller blades, lawnmower, leaf blower, skateboard, vacuum, broom, fan, umbrella, bridges, wet grass, snow, mud, balloons, various floor textures, and other friendly animals

Puppy Classes can be a great way to work on your puppy's socialization skills in a controlled environment with a good coach along your side. A good puppy class instructor will teach you how to introduce your puppy safely to new environments, including other dogs and people. For these reasons, the American Veterinary Society of Animal Behavior believes that a good puppy class should be the standard of care for puppies to receive proper puppy socialization before they are fully vaccinated.[6] The American Veterinary Society of Animal Behavior states, "Enrolling in puppy classes prior to three months of age can be an excellent means of improving training, strengthening the human-animal bond, and socializing puppies in an environment where risk of illness can be minimized." Dr. Ian Dunbar's rule of thumb is that a puppy should meet 100 new people before he is 3 months old.[7]

However, a puppy class that is not run well or with much management in puppy interactions can be detrimental to your puppy. Take your time when choosing the right dog trainer and puppy class. Ask your friends with friendly, social and well-behaved dogs who they recommend. Visit the dog trainer or dog training company's website and look for their training philosophy. Read it carefully. Do they explain exactly what methods are used and what methods will not be used? Check out their credentials and continuing education. Any good dog trainer is continually learning by attending seminars, reading books and obtaining hands-on experience. Call or email any trainers who seem well-versed in positive reinforcement dog training, have a good background in continuing education pertaining to dog behavior and teaching, and have experience to back up those claims. After you have spoken with them, if you feel comfortable, see if you can observe a class or a class video. When you are watching, you should be looking for humans and dogs who are relaxed and enjoying themselves.

Proper introductions to other dogs is an important part of your puppy's socialization process. Once again, you will want to ensure the best possible outcome you can during puppy to dog or puppy to puppy interactions. If you have another dog at home, it is still very imperative to continue teaching your puppy how to meet other dogs safely and appropriately. If your puppy is not correctly socialized with puppies and dogs of different sizes and breeds, he will be likely to develop behavior problems associated with dogs. Puppies do not come preprogrammed with proper doggie etiquette. It will be your job to teach your puppy in a safe manner how to politely greet and interact with other canines.

Introducing Your Puppy To Familiar Dogs/Puppies This is the perfect time to call on
your friends with dogs. But it is crucial to look for dog-friendly and puppy-friendly dogs. You do not want your puppy to be a guinea pig in finding out if another dog is puppy-friendly. **Puppy-friendly** dogs are dogs who can tolerate a puppy jumping on their head, running around in circles, and even

barking in their face. These puppy behaviors are very inappropriate dog greeting behaviors, which is why you are going to teach your puppy the proper skills in dog greeting. However, you want to help make certain that if a puppy mistake happens, the other dog can tolerate it and not hurt or scare your puppy.

- ❑ When you have found a puppy friendly dog the ideal meeting place will be outside. Pick a neutral location which can even be just a few houses down from either one of your homes. Plan on meeting on opposite sides of the street. With your puppy leashed to his front clipping harness, and some high-value treats in your pocket start to walk up and down the street about 3-5 houses in length. At the same time, your friend is doing the same with her dog on the opposite side of the street.

- ❑ Once it seems like both dogs are unresponsive to the other dog, have your friend and her dog come over to your side of the street 5 houses away and start to walk in the OPPOSITE direction. As your friend starts to walk, you walk your puppy behind. After a couple of houses, both of you change directions, so her dog is following your puppy.

- ❑ When each dog is once again not concerned with the other, start to close the distance between the two dogs until eventually your friend's dog gets the opportunity to smell your puppy's rear area. While this is happening, slip your hand inside your puppy's harness and feed him treats. This process will do a few things. First, it will help your puppy keep 4 on the floor and focused on you. Once a little sniffing has occurred, switch smelling positions and allow your puppy to smell the other dog's rear area.

- ❑ Once they both feel comfortable with each other, allow them to sniff each other for a few seconds, then call your puppy to you and give him a treat. This will allow your puppy to learn how to come off of other dogs, and will help keep the new canine interactions low key and more likely successful. Repeat the process of allowing the dogs to come together for little sniffing, and then calling them off of each other. Building the length of time they get to spend with each other.

- ❑ You can repeat this process, but more speeded up with each following interaction with the same dog. Each time you meet a new familiar dog, continue with the steps outlined. You will likely also be able to speed it up as your puppy learns the routine you are teaching him. But always continue to call your puppy off of interactions and give a high-value treat. This will come in handy in the future, so let the training begin now.
  - ❖ If your puppy is uncomfortable at any time, remove the two dogs. Do not keep your puppy there if he is not happy.
  - ❖ If either dog has any issue with the food or reacts in an unfriendly way, remove the dogs from each other.
  - ❖ Going for walks together with other dogs is a great way for your puppy to learn to interact with other dogs.

There will likely be a time in your puppy's life that he will actually have the opportunity for a playmate for the afternoon. Provide the same introduction as above. When it is time to retire to your home or another friend's home with both dogs, walk into the house or fenced in yard one dog after the other.

When your puppy is playing with other dogs, it is important to supervise play sessions to ensure they are playing safely and appropriately, so you must watch and intervene when needed. Appropriate play can quickly get out of hand and turn into aggression, particularly for dogs during adolescence since they are in the learning stages of self-control. This is one of the main reasons for teaching your puppy how to come off of other dogs. During appropriate play between the two dogs, occasionally call your puppy to you and give him a high-value treat. Do this before either dog gets too aroused and rough to keep both dogs' arousal in check by creating pauses and breaks in play. Over time, your puppy will likely learn how to take play breaks on his own. **Tip:** Listen and watch your puppy during play. To help you determine if the play is tipping toward over arousal look for changes in play style, louder, rougher, body slamming or more chaotic are some examples.

- ❑ If there is a spat during play, try not to get too worried. Calmly break them up and remove them from each other. Attach each dog to their coordinating leash and harness for a little time out and rest.
- ❑ If you have enrolled in a good puppy class, or are working with a good private dog trainer, they can help you with understanding dog body language and will be able to help guide you down the right path. It is always a good idea to have a qualified coach on your team.

Introducing Your Puppy To <u>Unfamiliar</u> Dogs/Puppies

This can be a bit trickier. When considering saying hello to an unfamiliar dog, first see how is that dog responding to their owner. If the dog is jumping around and pulling their owner across the sidewalk, then I would not advise saying hello to this dog. If, on the other hand, the dog looks well-behaved, with loose body language, then that dog might be a good candidate. But it is also important to realize not all dogs like other dogs and a larger portion of dogs do not appreciate puppies.

- ❑ Stop about 10' away from the other dog and owner and ask the owner if their dog likes PUPPIES. Again, it is imperative that the dog has good puppy experience. If they reply they do not know, or no, then thank them and keep walking. If on the other hand they positively respond, ask if they can say hello.
- ❑ Once the other owner gives you permission to say hello, walk your puppy off to the side about 5' and slowly walk toward the other owner and their dog. Keep your puppy's leash loose and occasionally ask for your puppy's attention and give him a treat for paying attention to you. You can help your puppy keep 4 on the floor by squatting down with your puppy and placing your hand in your puppy's harness so you can help maneuver your puppy to ensure he does not jump on the other dog's head.
- ❑ After a little sniffing, thank the owner and get your puppy's attention and calmly walk off.
  - ❖ If at anytime during the greeting you are unsure if the behavior of either dog is appropriate, thank the owner and leave. This is not the time to roll the dice.

Puppies And Children

Two of my personal favorite things in life are dogs and children. I know that some of you may think I am nuts, but I truly adore a good relationship between these two playful creatures. A relationship with the family dog can be one of our fondest memories as a child; I know it was mine. But it can also be a memory of stress, anxiety, injury, or even fatality. Dogs are after all, very strong predators with razor sharp teeth. If you have children, it is crucial to teach both your puppy and your children how to properly and safely interact with each other. If you do not have children, it is still important to teach your puppy these skills.

Just because your puppy is brought up with children does not mean that your puppy will behave around them, enjoy their company, or love all children. If your puppy has what he views as bad experiences with children (scary running, screaming, pulling his ears, hugging him, taking his toys), he can easily resent them and even become a danger to your children. Raising puppies and children together is a big responsibility on your part. I do want to repeat that: a **big** responsibility on **your** part. Once you decided to bring a puppy into your household, you are accountable for that puppy's life and his behavior, and this should not be taken lightly. In 2013, family dogs consisted of 47% of all fatal dog attacks. 78% of those attacks happened on the dog owner's property. 56% of the fatality victims were children under seven years of age.[8]

Active supervision and being proactive is a must. Actively supervising your puppy and children means that you are engaging and interacting with both. This means helping your child properly pet your puppy, teaching your child and puppy how to safely and appropriately play together, or teaching them to do tricks with each other. Actively supervising means you are **hands on**, not sitting in a chair belting out commands.

If you are not able to be hands on, then you should be proactive in using a management tool. Children who need to be told what to do or not do, over and over again, are not mature enough to have unsupervised access to the puppy. There is no magic age; it truly is about your child's reliability and your puppy's behavior. You can use management tools to keep your children and puppy separated. Items like baby gates, crates, and closed doors are perfect in these situations.

Children and puppy guidelines to get you started.
- ❏ **Being Gentle, Calm and Kind-**Teaching your children to be kind and gentle can go a long way in the success of a harmonious household. The same holds true for your puppy. Teaching your puppy to take treats nicely, keep four on the floor and not to be rowdy around your children leads to a more successful relationship. Remember, you will be actively supervising and engaging the two, so you will be able to teach both how to interact properly with each other.
- ❏ **Training-**Involve your children in some of the puppy training, once your puppy understands a cue. For example, once you have taught your puppy to sit on cue, work with your child on teaching the puppy to sit on cue for them. The same goes for other behaviors and tricks such as down, stay, spin and touch. This allows two things to happen. One, your child is appropriately interacting with the puppy; and two, the puppy is learning to listen and follow cues from your child.
- ❏ **Play-**Teaching your child and puppy how to play together appropriately is important. Once again you have two creatures with a high play drive, and you want to ensure both of their safety. Rowdy games are not appropriate for children and dogs to play together. Instead, you want to teach calm and cooperative games such as fetch, find the toy, and toy challenge. See *Games To Play With Your Puppy pg. 18*
- ❏ **Going For A Walk-**Going for an outside walk is definitely a family adventure. Even if your children are old enough that they do not need active supervision, so much can happen out in public. First, your puppy can become excited and slip through your child's hands and get lost, or worse, killed by a car. Second, a lot of people do not abide by leash laws, and their dogs are not always dog-friendly. I have personally known two children who ran into this situation and the outcome was very traumatic. Instead of risking the unforeseen, use this walk as a family bonding opportunity where you accompany your child.
- ❏ **Do Not Pick Up the Puppy-**Do not allow your child, or anyone else for that matter, to pick up your puppy. First, many people pick puppies up incorrectly by their front legs or arms and can severely injury the puppy. Second, a puppy can get squirmy or mouthy, and people have been known just to let go and drop the puppy. Third, puppies can be scared of the approach, lift up, or height.
- ❏ **Do Not Bother the Puppy-**You should teach your children to leave the puppy alone when he is eating, sleeping, chewing or in his crate. These are not times for your child to try to engage your puppy in activity.

- **Safety Zones**-To increase your chances of a successful integration of your puppy and children, set up puppy-free zones and kid-free zones. In other words, places in your home that your children can be kids and run around, leave toys on the floor, scream and be a kid where the puppy cannot enter. The same rule goes for the puppy: He also gets a place where he can rest or retreat that children will not bother him. One of the ways you can accomplish this is by utilizing baby gates. If your child's room is a dog free room, place a swinging baby gate on the door so your child can enter and your puppy cannot. If your puppy's kid free space is the laundry room with his crate and water dish, teach your children not to enter that room when your puppy is there. Remember to remind your children continually about the *Do Not Bother the Puppy* rule.
- **Your Children's Friends**-Please keep in mind that these tips are promoting active supervision. This is doubly true when you have other kids over. There is no room for error when you are talking about the safety of children. Depending on the friend, sometimes it is best to use an active management tool and not allow your puppy access to the friend. Each situation is different, and you should always err on the side of caution.

For those people who do not have their own children, it is important to work actively on a socialization plan to introduce your puppy to a variety of children and age ranges. The same goes for parents with children. Your children are different than "strange" children. Keep in mind you want your puppy to enjoy the experience, so take it slow and do not rush into a crowd of screaming kids, look for quiet, friendly children playing at the playground. Ask their parents if it is okay to introduce your puppy. Review the section *People In Public pg. 38* on how to keep your puppy's four feet on the floor during greeting.

Puppy Etiquette Being a responsible puppy parent not only entails raising a happy dog, but being courteous of the general public. When you take your puppy out in public, you are looking for an enjoyable experience with your puppy. The same holds true for other dog parents and non-dog people. Here are some simple guidelines on how you and your puppy can be valued community members.

- Pick up after your puppy 100% of the time. When you are out and about with your puppy, bring at least five poop bags. Nobody wants to step in dog poop.
- Respect people and other dog's space. I know it may be hard to believe, but not everyone wants to say hello to your cute little puppy, and the same goes for other dogs. If you want to say hello to someone, please stop about five feet away and ask. Please respect their choice if they say, "no."
- Keep your puppy on a leash in all outside areas unless the location is a dedicated off-leash dog area. Too many things can go wrong in a split second. Plus, a lot of people and other dogs do not want a dog to rush up to them, friendly or not.
- Teach and train your puppy to behave in public places.

Handling, Restraint and Grooming As early as possible, you should start to get your puppy comfortable with being handled, restrained and groomed. You will frequently be grooming your puppy's coat, wiping his feet, brushing his teeth, reaching for him quickly, trimming his nails and even possibly removing a thorn from his foot pad. These reoccurring actions can be quite challenging if you do not teach your puppy now how to enjoy being handling and to be calm and relaxed during handling and grooming. In these *daily exercises,* you will be teaching your puppy to trust you and to view these procedures as enjoyable and not stressful. For detailed instructions on how to brush, bathe and give your puppy a nail trim, read the section on *Brushing, Bathing, Nail Trims and Dental Care pg. 47*

- ❑ Hold your puppy's collar then give him a treat.
- ❑ Pick up your puppy's front foot then give him a treat. Repeat with each foot, his tail and ears.
- ❑ Lift your puppy's lip and give him a treat.
- ❑ Gently stroke the top of your puppy's head and give him a treat.
- ❑ Gently hug your puppy and give him a treat.
- ❑ Take a soft brush and stroke your puppy's back and give him a treat.
- ❑ Repeat these steps with various family members, friends, and strangers.
  - ❖ As your puppy starts to look forward to these lessons start to increase the length of your touching. For example, instead of picking up your puppy's front paw and treating, pick up your puppy's paw and hold for a couple of seconds, then treat. You are working toward longer duration so that you can examine your puppy's body, give nail trims, pull out possible thorns, etc.
  - ❖ If your puppy is being mouthy during any of these lessons, do a little less before giving the treat. You can also allow him to lick a food stuffed hollow treat toy during handling.
  - ❖ Remember, your puppy must view all this as enjoyable. If he seems cautious on any of these things, proceed very slowly, or contact a professional.

Do not get complacent in handling your puppy. It is critical to remember that puppies go through many changes in the first 18 months of their lives. Even though your puppy may be fine with it now, this does not guarantee that he will be fine later in life. Practice these exercises on a daily basis, and remember to reward heavily for good behavior.

Relaxation Techniques Teaching your puppy how to relax on cue is a tool that you can use on a regular basis. It is designed to teach your puppy self-control. If practiced on a regular basis, your puppy will learn how to stay still for extended periods of time. Teaching this technique takes time and patience, but pays off in the end.

- ❑ Begin in a quiet location on a soft surface.
- ❑ Make sure you are going to be distraction-free.
- ❑ Get yourself a comfortable cushion to sit on and maybe turn on your favorite TV program.
- ❑ Put your puppy's harness and leash on.
- ❑ Bring your puppy close to your body.
- ❑ Slowly and steadily rub his chest in a circular motion.
- ❑ Calmly rub his entire body starting at the base of his head and working your way down to his tail and feet.
- ❑ You may want to speak soothingly to your puppy.
- ❑ As you are gently massaging your puppy, you are also evaluating his skin and body. This is an excellent time to keep a watch for lumps, growths or anything out of the ordinary that may develop.
- ❑ After a few minutes, calmly release your puppy. Make sure he is relaxed prior to releasing him. Over time, you can steadily increase the duration your puppy is sitting calmly with you.
- ❑ As he progresses, try this technique during more distracting times such as when guests are over, or at the park.

Games To Play With Your Puppy

Puppies are very playful creatures and continue to enjoy play throughout their adult lives. I would imagine that is one of the reasons you brought a puppy into your home: to have a companion to spend time with and enjoy. Building a good play relationship with your puppy can greatly enhance your relationship and bond. By becoming a good play partner, you will become more important and valuable to your puppy. In turn, they will prefer to be with you and will listen better.

To help increase your puppy's manners, do not play with your puppy when he is demanding attention. Instead, offer play sessions when he is being good. Play sessions ideally will be short and sweet and speckled often throughout your day. By asking your puppy to play often, he is less likely to be demanding about getting attention.

Play is a great way to teach your puppy emotional control. During your play sessions, take frequent pauses in order to teach this important life skill to your puppy. For example, if you are playing a game of fetch, before the fifth toss of the ball, hold the ball close to your chest, wait for your puppy to offer a sit behavior (*Sit pg. 31*), count to 5, then toss. Vary the time between pauses, and vary the time your puppy waits before the toss. If he jumps up and gets excited, do not say anything, just wait for him to offer that sit behavior. By doing this, you are teaching your puppy to think for himself, and think through the process of controlling his own actions and emotions. If you are always "telling him" what to do, he will not learn to control himself. To continue your puppy's emotional control, after a play session give your puppy something to chew on and occupy himself with, so he understands that you are done playing, and he can appropriately focus on something else. Review *Safe Dog Chews and Bones pg. 45*

Inappropriate play relationships can have the opposite effect on the relationship. You will want to teach your puppy ways to play with humans. Those ways are different than the ways two canines play together. Inappropriate play behaviors between puppies and humans include body slamming, biting, mouthing, jumping, wrestling or teasing. Playing and spending time with your puppy should be the highlight of your day, not a battle.

Here are a few appropriate puppy games to get you started.
- ❑ **Find The Toy**-Start by playing with one of your puppy's favorite toys. Get a nice game going. Ask him to Sit/Stay (or hold him back if he does not know it), and place the toy 5' from him and say, "Find It!" Once he grabs it, start playing again. Build on this game, putting the toy farther away. **Tip:** If your dog can stay while you leave the room, place the toy in another room as you tell him, "Find It!" You can encourage him as he looks for the toy.
    - ❖ **Variation**-Find you! Ask your puppy to stay as you leave the room and tuck yourself behind something. Once you are hidden, quickly say your puppy's name then be quiet. Let him look around for you. Give him a chance to find you. If he has a real hard time finding you, make a little noise. When he finds you, make a big fuss and play. If he does not have a stay, you can hide when he is not paying attention, or drop a few treats on the floor and run away.
- ❑ **Toy Challenge**-Playing with your puppy does not have to be structured. You can wing it. Grab one of your puppy's favorite toys (or food treat if needed) and toss it under a blanket on the floor with just a part of the toy sticking out. Encourage your puppy to get it and when he does make a big fuss. Build on this behavior until the toy is totally covered, then build until you wrap the toy up a few times in the blanket.

❖ **Variation**-Put the toy or treat in something like a box or your laundry basket. If your puppy knows a good stay, put different toys in different places (with him watching and staying) then go to each hiding spot with him and encourage him to get the toy and move to the next toy.

❑ **Sniffy-Sniffy**-If your puppy likes to smell the roses this will be a very exciting and rewarding way to interact with your puppy. Go outside with your puppy and teach him to sniff on cue. Get excited, say "sniffy-sniffy" and point and touch the ground. Point to something that is likely to have some interest, like a mole hole or tree trunk, and encourage your puppy to check out the area. Let him lead the way, then say sniffy-sniffy again, pointing to something else fun and exciting. Wow! Your puppy is going to love you for engaging him in sniffing. And if you are actively pointing out random sniff spots, he will think you are so cool at finding the best smells around. **Tip:** I use this sniffing cue as a life reward for good behavior during a walk.

❑ **Chase Me**-Puppies love movement and are almost always up for a good game of chase. The best chase game is teaching your puppy to chase you. Chasing your puppy could lead to some come-when-called issues, so I do not recommend it for beginners. If you are really fun, rolling on the ground will get your puppy even more interested in the game. Start by saying your puppy's name in a sing-song tone and bend, turn and move away from your puppy quickly, but do not go too far too fast so he can not catch you. When he does catch you tell him how smart he is. You can reward with some attention, petting, food, or even another run away. **Tip:** This is a great game to play outside to build his attention on you with all those distractions. You will be teaching him that you are fun and valuable. You can also throw in some sit behaviors when he catches up to you, increasing his manners.

❑ **Fetch and Drop**-Is a wonderful cooperative game to play with your puppy. A game of fetch with the puppy is a great game for kids to play once your puppy is reliable in the rules of the game. Have two identical toys, such as two balls. Toss one of the balls about 5' away from your puppy. When your puppy runs back with the first ball, wiggle the second ball in front of him trying to get him excited about it. As soon as he drops the first ball, toss the second ball that you had in your hand. Repeat this process. When your puppy is quickly returning and dropping the ball, say your drop or give cue right before he drops the ball.

❑ **Training**-Believe it or not, all these "games" you are playing are actually training lessons. If your puppy thinks you are fun, engaging and valuable, he is more likely to listen to you and **WANT** to be with you. That is the best foundation in training your puppy. A recent study determined that a play session before structured training lessons increased a dog's attentiveness during training.[9] So have fun and get out and play with your puppy every day. Training and play sessions should not be very long. Keep everything short and sweet so that your puppy is still engaged, so have sessions a few minutes to 20 minutes long, several times during the day.

Preventing Common Behavioral Problems

Preventing Thunder Phobia BANG! For many years when I heard the crack of thunder I knew I was going to be in for a long night (or day). My golden retriever Theo had developed thunder phobia in 2001. I do not mean he was a little nervous when he heard the rumbles of a storm, I mean Theo wanted to dig to China, crawl inside me, eat his way out of the house and at times I thought he was just going to explode! It was awful for him, me, and the entire family.

Thunder phobia in dogs is one of the hardest behavioral issues to treat in dogs, particularly if you live in a place where storms are frequent. Unfortunately, we cannot tell the storm, "Okay, that's enough, not so loud" and control the intensity like we can with a lot of other behavioral problems. A thunder-phobic dog is continually being pushed past his comfort zone and threshold, making it a very complex situation to manage and treat.

Theo has since passed (2009), and to this day, my fingers still start to tingle with a bit of anxiety when I hear that first boom. But then I look down at my current dog, Dexter, snoozing away, oblivious to it all, and I can go back to sleep.

At the beginning of this booklet, I touched on preventing behavioral problems in your puppy. I will now focus on preventing thunder phobia in your puppy. Believe me, you do not want your puppy to develop thunder phobia. Thunder phobia is extremely hard to treat in dogs. You will be best served to work hard on a prevention protocol now rather than try to deal with a phobia in the future.

Prevention, prevention, prevention! When you are blessed with a puppy who does not have an issue with a common behavior problem such as storm phobia, it is important to keep that response. My students often say, "but he's fine in a storm," I'm thrilled, I really am, but fear can develop anytime in a dog's life. In order to help buffer any future phobias, now is the time to develop the "no worries" attitude with storms. We are building habits and emotional responses to things (storms in this lesson), so it takes a lot of repetition to get our famous Pavlov response working.

Preventing thunder phobia in dogs does not take a lot of work on your part. But it does take a bit of planning and good timing on your execution. It is a multi-faceted approach. I will outline some of the things you can do to prevent this devastating anxiety in your puppy.

Exercise #1 Always work *below* your puppy's anxiety levels. If you see any signs of anxiety (darting eyes, panting, restlessness, clinginess, etc.), it's too much. You need to make it less stressful (usually quieter).

Get some high-value treat rewards. High-value is something your dog goes crazy over (review ***Motivation pg. 2***). I usually start by looking for meat products, such as cooked beef, salmon or lean pork. We need to make a real impact here, instead of using a regular dog biscuit or dog kibble.

Find various recorded storm sounds. You can purchase thunderstorm CDs, or use my favorite these days, YouTube. One important aspect here is to make sure you use different tracks, so it's different at each lesson.

Do not let your puppy see you grab the high-value dog treats or prepare your thunderstorm recording. You want this to feel real, not set up. Turn your recording on with the volume very, very low. I do not want you to scare your puppy! Be ready. As soon as you hear a little rumble, toss your dog a tiny piece of treat. Repeat with the next rumble. *Do not worry if now your dog is at your feet. You can smile at him, but just keep tossing the treats when you hear that rumble or boom! Even if he starts to offer other behaviors, barking, sitting, shaking, you are just going to ignore those.* Repeat this process as often as you can think about it. Try changing locations/rooms and do not forget to change that track! You do not always have to be sitting down either to do it. Remember, we want your dog to think this is normal.

Exercise #2-The Real Deal Ok, the real storm (or hopefully just a little rain and rumble) is here! Just like in your previous exercises, we are conditioning your dog that the rumbles and booms of thunder predict good things. Crazy good things! Each rumble....toss of treat. Just like before. The difference is, you won't be able to predict how loud those booms are going to be. So, if it's pretty loud, I usually jackpot. Treat, treat, treat. Wow!

What if this storm is happening at 3am? Yes, you guessed it; I grab the peanut butter jar, and give a lick after each rumble. *I highly recommend watching the weather stations to know when those storms are going to happen. Again, you want to be prepared. Believe me, doing this at 3am a few times is worth it. If your dog develops thunder phobia, you WILL be up at 3am for storms.*

Alternative Rewarding System. There have been dogs who respond well to a good game of play during a storm as a way of prevention. However, I typically prefer to do more rewarding after a boom, and maybe some play pre- and post-storm. But if you have a crazy play driven puppy, this may be a good route. The same goes for a continual reward during a storm like chewing on a high value stuffed rubber toy. But again, we are not targeting the booms quite as much. But I have been known to reward for booms for say 1/2 hour, then give a stuffed chew toy for the remainder of the storm and toss meat for booms too!

Preventing Resource Guarding In Dogs A very common and natural behavior in dogs is resource guarding. Resource guarding is a term commonly used that refers to a dog that uses threats to protect items that he sees as valuable. Dogs can deem any item, location, space, or person as a valuable possession worth fighting for. Resource guarding is a survival instinct and once again a normal dog behavior but not something we want to see in our pet dogs. You are best served to work on a prevention program instead of trying to deal with a behavior that can be very severe and even life-threatening. *If you are seeing signs of guarding, growling, or lunging around resources, please contact a professional for immediate help. Do not attempt these lessons without professional assistance if you are seeing signs of guarding.*

The Food Bowl You will be teaching your puppy that not only is it okay for a person to approach while he is eating out of his food bowl, but that it is a very good thing when they do. Of course, I am hoping you are using your puppy's food for training and interactive treat toys, and the below exercise, instead of using a bowl for meals.

- ❑ Approach empty bowl and puppy, put a small handful of food in and allow your puppy to eat the food. As he is eating add another handful of kibbles. Practice this session once a day for three days.
- ❑ Approach empty bowl and puppy, remove bowl, put a handful of food in, put the bowl back down and allow your puppy to eat the food. Before he is finished, put your hand inside the food bowl and drop three high-value treats inside and remove your hand. Practice this session once a day for three days.
- ❑ Approach empty bowl and puppy, remove bowl, put a handful of food in, put the bowl back down and allow your puppy to eat the food. Before he is finished, pick up the bowl add more kibbles and a few pieces of meat treats in the bowl then set back down for him to eat. Practice this session once a day for three days.
- ❑ Approach empty bowl and puppy, put the entire meal of food in the bowl, put the bowl back down and allow your puppy to eat the food. Before he is finished, place a handful of meat treats inside of his bowl. Practice this session once a day for three days.
- ❑ Approach empty bowl and puppy, put the entire meal of food in the bowl, put the bowl back down and allow your puppy to eat the food. Leave the room, come back into the room and pick up the bowl and place a handful of meat treats inside his bowl and place back down. Practice this session once a day for three days. After your three days, repeat this process every other day for a week, then once a week for his entire life to keep the behavior and reaction strong.

Bone, Chew, Or Toy It is important to remember you are working on a *prevention* program and teaching your puppy how to live safely in a human world. Even if your puppy is not showing signs of guarding (I hope he is not), practice these approaches throughout his adolescence.
- ❑ Approach your puppy while he is chewing a bone or toy, and drop a couple of meat treats right at his feet and chew toy and walk away. Repeat this exercise five times throughout your day as you see your puppy interacting with his bones and toys. Practice this session for three days.
- ❑ Approach your puppy while he is chewing a bone or toy, remove the bone or chew and smear peanut butter, or squirt cheese on chew and return it back to your puppy. Repeat this exercise five times throughout your day as you see your puppy interacting with his bones and toys. Practice this session for three days. If your puppy has his toy, when you remove the toy return the toy to him with a handful of meat treats.

Stolen Objects If your puppy has the opportunity to steal items you would rather he didn't have, you should look back at your management plan. Parenting your puppy takes a lot of work and can be quite challenging. Having your management in place can aid in less stress on your part and your puppy learning appropriate home behavior. However, when life happens and your puppy snags something he should not have, below are the steps to prevent him from guarding his find. Remember, you want to teach him it is okay for you to take his things. So even if you do not want him to have it, you should do a trade to get it back and increase your management to prevent it from happening in the future.
- ❑ Approach your puppy with the stolen item and toss a handful of meat treats at his feet. Calmly remove the item and put it in a location where your puppy cannot retrieve it again.

Being on Furniture If you are going to allow your puppy access to furniture there should be a few rules involved.
- ❑ Your puppy should allow you to remove him without a fuss.
- ❑ You should be able to slip your hand in his collar without a fuss.
- ❑ He should not be showing guarding signs toward people in any scenarios.

If the above three rules are not followed, your puppy has not earned the privilege of being on the furniture. If he has met these rules, you will want to follow a prevention program to keep this behavior strong and not to develop a future incident.

- ❑ Approach your puppy while he is resting on the furniture and hand him a meat treat. Practice this session various times throughout the day for three days.
- ❑ Approach your puppy while he is resting on the furniture and place your hand inside his collar and hand him a meat treat. Practice this session various times throughout the day for three days.
- ❑ Approach your puppy while he is resting on the furniture and place your hand inside his collar and ask him to get off the furniture as you gently guide him off. Once he is off hand him a meat treat. Practice this session various times throughout the day for three days.

People Some puppies have a tendency to bond very strongly to one person. Such a bond can develop into resource-guarding in the future. Your puppy should learn to share their attention with other people and other dogs. Puppies are pretty quick at making simple associations; therefore, you want to make sure you are giving him the right association.

- ❑ Sit on the floor or sofa if allowed on the furniture with your puppy. Have another family member come in and sit on the other side of you so that you are in the middle of your puppy and the family member. When your family member sits down, give your puppy a treat. Practice this session five times throughout the day for one day.
- ❑ Sit on the floor or sofa if allowed on the furniture with your puppy. Have another family member come in and sit on the other side of you so that you are in the middle of your puppy and the family member. When your family member sits down, give each other a hug, then give your puppy a treat. Practice this session five times throughout the day for one day.
- ❑ Sit on the floor or sofa if allowed on the furniture with your puppy. Have another family member come in and give you a hug, then give your puppy a treat. Practice this session five times throughout the day for one day.

Tips and Reminders
- ❑ Start each exercise over with a new adult doing the exercises, providing no aggression or guarding has occurred.
- ❑ Resource guarding is a behavior that can occur at any age, at any time. Therefore, it is essential to work on prevention throughout your puppy's life through old age.
- ❑ If you have small children it is critical teach them at an early age not to bother the puppy while he is chewing, eating, or sleeping. Do not allow children to see you perform these exercises, as kids tend to do as they see, not as they are told.
- ❑ ***If you ever see your puppy stiffen up, growl, or snap, stop your exercises and seek professional help immediately.***

Preventing Separation Anxiety Separation anxiety in dogs is a condition where a dog exhibits distress when left alone. It is estimated that 20-40% of dogs seen by animal behavior practices in North America suffer from separation anxiety.[10] Most dogs with separation anxiety start to show distress when their owners start their departure routine. A dog can go into a full-blown panic, be destructive to themselves or to the things around them. They may eliminate, eat walls, shake, drool, or even jump through windows.

It is essential to teach your puppy how to cope with being left alone. Already, your puppy probably can predict when it is dinner time, time to go outside, or when you are about to leave. If you stop to think about it, you usually perform certain sequences of events prior to these activities, and you can take action now to help prevent separation anxiety.

Be unpredictable! If you are continually varying your routine, your puppy will not be able to anticipate your comings and goings. We have heard numerous times, "dogs love a routine," but some dogs are not able to handle it if a routine is broken.

- ❑ **Quiet Comings and Goings**-It is important that when you come home, and leave for the day, you are not overly excited greeting your puppy. If you make a big deal about your coming and going, your puppy will begin to think that it must be traumatic to be left alone. A simple, but warm hello and good-bye with a scratch and smile is best.
- ❑ **Vary Your Daily Routine**-Change the time you get up in the morning, change the sequence of your morning routine, even if it is only by fifteen minutes.
- ❑ **Spending Time Alone**-One of the toughest things for new puppy parents is to allow their puppy time to rest in their crate or another out-of-sight spot when they are home. But allowing your puppy quiet time alone will help him learn that it is okay if he is not by your side all the time. Review *Crate Training Exercises pg. 7* for details and practice alone time two to three times a day.
- ❑ **Exercise and Human Play**-A tired puppy is a good puppy that is ready for naps and rest. Proper exercise can positively affect your puppy's mood and behavior. Exercise before your departures can be helpful, but it is important that the exercise is low-impact and you allow your puppy a cool down period before leaving. If not, you may get the opposite result and have a more energetic puppy when you leave.

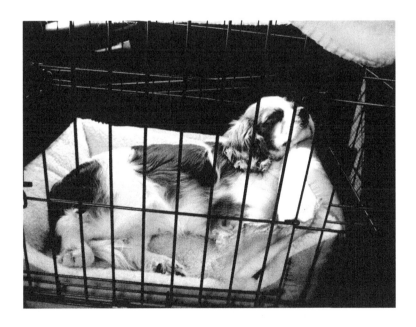

Potty Training

One necessary behavior you will want to teach your puppy is to eliminate in the appropriate place. The appropriate place should be outside. I do not recommend teaching your puppy to use potty pads or any other indoor pee space, because they teach your puppy it is okay to eliminate indoors. The second part in effective potty training is to teach your puppy to hold it until he is allowed outside. When you first start to tackle potty training, you must first be aware of a few key factors.

Age The average puppy does not have the capacity in his bladder to "hold" all his urine until he is about 4-5 months of age. The same goes for his mind to control the urge of going potty when he feels the stress of his bladder when getting full. Their bladders are typically developed at full size around 7 months of age.

Puppies need to go out many times a day. Their bladders are small, and need to be emptied out after activities. You will need to take your puppy outside after playing, chewing their bones, running around, eating, drinking a lot of water, sleeping, and of course every time you see him doing a circling motion or seemig restless. It's not uncommon to take an active puppy out every 15 minutes. But, do not worry, this is just temporary.

When you take your puppy out to eliminate, you will need to stay with him. When he goes to the bathroom outside, let him know he is being a good boy by praising him and giving him a treat. This should take place where he is going potty, not after he comes inside. You can introduce your potty word by saying, "go potty" just as he is about to eliminate. After he finishes, tell him how good he is, and give him his treat and some love.

After you have praised your puppy for going potty outside, DO NOT TAKE HIM BACK IN THE HOUSE! This will only cause your puppy to delay going potty, because he does not want to go back inside. Instead, play a quick little game with your puppy outside. One exception, of course, is if he *wants* to go back inside.

Supervision You must actively watch and supervise your puppy very closely. You may even want to attach him to you by a leash clipped to your belt, attached to your chair, or under your foot. This way he can never just disappear and go potty in a corner. When you are not able to keep a constant eye on him a wise idea is to put your puppy in his crate. Preventing mistakes is the best tool in training. Use it consistently.

Asking to go out or bell training is not something I recommend. Both of these behaviors can become very demanding, and puppies quickly learn that asking to go out or ringing the bell allows them to go out and play and chase critters around the yard. The purpose of going out to eliminate disappears. That is not to say if your puppy is obviously standing by the potty door you should not take him out, because of course you should. Just do not require your puppy to "tell you" when he has to go. Be actively taking him out when *you* think he needs to go.

Accidents Catching a potty mistake is not the end of the world. Remember he is a puppy, and accidents will happen. What you do when this happens is very important. When you catch your puppy in the act, calmly say NO, scoop him up and rush him outside. Do not reprimand him, or he will likely just learn not to potty in front of you. If he finishes eliminating outside, praise him for eliminating in the right spot.

Do not scold your puppy for eliminating in the house if you did not see the crime. It is too late, and they will not understand why they are being punished. Rubbing their nose in it only confuses them. Instead, put him in his crate and clean up the mess.

Clean Up You must remove the odor completely, or your puppy will think that is an appropriate place to eliminate. Do not use vinegar or cleaners containing ammonia. These will only attract your puppy back to the spot. Instead use enzymatic cleaner. Baking soda or club soda will also neutralize the odor.

Mouthing People

Teaching your new puppy not to mouth, gnaw, or bite people is one of the fundamental behaviors in raising a polite puppy. What may seem cute, or fun now, can become a serious behavioral problem in the future. Puppies are very mouthy and do a lot of chewing and biting. As you parent your puppy, you will be teaching him what is appropriate to chew and bite on. It is never appropriate to bite or chew on people or their shoes or clothing.

Make sure everyone follows these simple rules; dogs do not understand they can do something with one person, but not with another. I hate to be sexist, but the men in the family are typically the ones who initiate rough, mouthy behavior during play, but this is not appropriate play behavior between puppies and humans. You will be teaching your puppy it is NOT okay to place their mouth or teeth on any part of any human, including their clothing.

The Right Chew Toys
- ❑ Have plenty of acceptable puppy toys around for your puppy to access. You will want these toys easily accessible, and at least 5 -10 in each of the main rooms the puppy resides in.
- ❑ Do not use household items as toys. Your puppy may end up thinking your favorite shoes are his toys.
- ❑ Have a variety of bully sticks, hollow rubber treat toys, soft rubber toys, plush toys and fleece tug ropes. Keep in mind you will be actively supervising your puppy and his toys to make sure they are appropriate and safe for him. Puppies have different play and chew styles. You do not want your puppy to break pieces off his toy and eat them. If he does, please throw them away and try a new toy or company. You do not want to take the chance that a piece may get lodged in his intestine. Surgery is much more expensive than a new toy.

Encourage Your Puppy To Chew And Play With His Toys
- ❑ If your puppy is not interested in his new chew or rubber bone, try soaking it in organic chicken or beef broth for 24 hours, or smudge a little peanut butter or squirt cheese on it to initiate some interest.
- ❑ Praise your puppy every time you notice him playing with his toys while he is still learning, to teach him that it is a good thing to chew on the right items.
- ❑ Once your puppy has successfully learned what is appropriate to chew and play with you only have to praise him occasionally when he is chewing on his toys.

What To Do If He Mouths You
- ❑ If your puppy starts to mouth you, say a quick "ouch" as you remove your hand and place your hand tight against your chest.
- ❑ If you are on the floor, or were squatting down, immediately stand straight, fold your arms, turn your back and ignore your puppy. A mouthing puppy = an invisible puppy. Do not talk to him, do not tell him no, just ignore him. No attention.
- ❑ Once your puppy is calmer, you can calmly praise and interact with him again.
- ❑ If your puppy does it again, repeat the process. This is important because he is learning that if he does mouth you, you will continue to ignore him and when he is calm, you will give him attention. If it continues, call a time out. Say "Too Bad," and walk away and do something else. He will soon learn that his behavior caused you to walk away.

- If he is really acting up and jumping and mouthing, walk into another room and shut the door behind you, leaving him in the other room. This sometimes really gets the message across. Wait a few seconds and return. Repeat as needed.

Tips and Reminders
- During playtime with your puppy, try to keep the play and arousal low-key. If your puppy gets too excited, it usually encourages mouthy behavior.
- Anticipating times of the day or behavior trends when your puppy tends to get more mouthy can be helpful. If you see a pattern, you can direct your puppy on the right toy, *before* he grabs your hand, clothing, or shoes.
- If your puppy is not getting the appropriate amount of interactive exercise or play with you, he will be more likely to offer undesirable mouthing behaviors.

The Name Game

Teaching a puppy the value of his name is one of the first lessons I start in a puppy program. When I say, "Dexter" that means for my dog Dexter to turn around and look at me, not for him to blow me off and ignore me. Your puppy's name should be a pleasant experience, not a punishment. In other words, good things happen to your dog when they hear their name.

I start to teach a dog **The Name Game** during a planned dog training session. In other words, not when you are distracted, or your dog is distracted by his environment. Start your set up without your dog seeing you "set up." Place 20-30 tiny high-value dog treats in your pocket. I say high value, and I mean something so exciting your dog will go crazy over, like cooked chicken, steak, beef....whatever gets him to drool excessively! Then also place a small toy, such as a squeaker toy in your other pocket.

Week 1
- ❑ Start your dog training session when your dog is already hanging out with you and not distracted.
- ❑ Say your puppy's name **ONE TIME** in a pleasant, high pitch sing-song voice.
- ❑ That moment when your dog turns his head to look at you, immediately mark that behavior with a "YES!", "Good!" or click if you are using a clicker.
- ❑ Follow quickly with a jackpot of 10 treats as you fuss over and praise him. Dish out the 10 treats quickly, but one at a time. You want him to feel like he just won the lottery!
- ❑ That's it! That is the fist stage in teaching your dog the value of his name. No distractions (not outside, not when he is barking, not when he is sleeping).....right now.
- ❑ Practice this 10 times a day at random times for one week. You want your dog to be successful, not blow off his name. So, in the meantime, do not call your dog with his name if you think you are going to get the blow off. You are probably re-teaching him what the true meaning of his name is.
    - ❖ **Oops!** He didn't look at you. Do not repeat his name, instead grab that squeaker toy you had in your pocket, start tossing it around and squeaking it while ignoring him. He does not get to play with it; you have a fun time with it by yourself. Grab his toy and go play with it yourself. Or whip out that tasty treat and pretend to eat it yourself.
    - ❖ Wait about 5 minutes and if you think your dog is not distracted, try the name game again. Assuming he turns this time, jackpot as usual. If he does not look toward you, revaluate the training environment. It is important that he wins at this level and often if you expect him to be able to do it with distractions.
    - ❖ **Tips and Bonuses**-When you practice a set, you can add more rewards after your jackpot to really bring it home. For example, after your 10 treats, he gets his dinner, or to play, go for a walk, Kong filled toy....get creative. A quick and reliable name game is a precursor to come-when-called and everything else involved with getting your puppy's attention on you and not his environment.

Week 2-After a successful week of practicing your puppy's name without any distractions, you should have at least 70 repetitions of saying your puppy's name, him turning and him receiving a wonderful jackpot and hopefully some bonus rewards too. If this does not seem like the case, keep working on your week 1 homework.
- ❑ Same rules as week 1, except this time you are going to start to add very mild distractions to your puppy's environment during your sessions. Again, you are looking for success, so be

careful not to ask for too much yet. If you are unsuccessful, try something a bit easier and reset.

❑ **Example**-Your dog is calmly engaged in another activity such as looking out the window, moving around the house, playing calmly with a low value toy.....get in about 5' away, say your puppy's name in that sing-song voice and that moment he looks toward you, your marker (Yes, Good, clicker) and jackpot of treats, 10 times a day!

Week 3 and Beyond-This is an ongoing training lesson. Over time and experience you can continue to build on your puppy's behavior and response to his name. If you start to lose him over time, decrease your criteria and rebuild again. If you want a reliable behavior, you will need to practice and to keep fresh in his head that great things happen with the calling of his name.

Basic Training Cues

Sit is a great behavior to teach all puppies right away. By teaching a reliable sit behavior, you will be able to ask your puppy to sit his butt down instead of jumping. Once your puppy understands the idea of sitting, you can ask your puppy to *offer a sit* when they want something like attention, food, toy playing or just about anything else. In these lessons, I will teach you the various steps in teaching your puppy to sit, and the various steps in teaching you to teach your puppy to offer the sit behavior without being asked.

Grab a handful of rewards and keep your lessons short (no more than 5 minutes at a time). Advance through levels when your puppy is mastering the session 5/5. At every new training session, go back a level when you start for the best success. If at anytime your puppy isn't successful, repeat the level or go back a level to get success.

Level 1
- ❑ Put the treat right to your puppy's nose, and move your hand slowly in an arc above your puppy's head and back
- ❑ As soon as his rump hits the floor say **"YES!"** and follow quickly with a treat. Repeat 5 times

Level 2
- ❑ Remove the food lure from your hand
- ❑ Make the same motion of luring your dog to a sit position
- ❑ As soon as his rump hits the floor say **"YES!"** and treat (treat was in your opposite hand). Repeat 5 times

Level 3
- ❑ Say your Sit cue just before you lure with your empty hand
- ❑ As soon as his rump hits the floor say **"YES!"** and treat (treat was in your opposite hand). Repeat 5 times

Level 4
- ❑ Do a rep of Level 3
- ❑ Now, on your next trial, say your Sit cue, without your hand lure
- ❑ As soon as your dog sits, say **"YES!"** and treat (treat was in your opposite hand). Repeat 5 times

Adding Distractions-when you are asking your puppy to work on his sit behavior around distractions such as being outside, around guests or other puppies, you must start the training process over at Level 1 and rebuild. Just because your puppy is performing his sit cue in the living room does not mean he can do the same behavior outside. He must learn this process just like he was learned it in the living room.

Offering The Sit After you have practiced various lessons with your puppy on the sit behavior, it's time to teach your puppy to read your mind! This is easier than it sounds. Do a round of Sit sessions. After, say, 3 sets, just smile at your puppy, do not provide any luring or words. As soon as his butt hits the floor say **"YES!"** and give him a jackpot of treats. Quickly take a few playful steps away from your puppy and stop and smile at him again. As soon as his butt hits the floor again, say "**YES!**" and treat. Repeat this for a total of 5 times.

You can vary the offered sit by doing the same process before other events that your puppy wants to participate in. For example, if you are about ready to toss your puppy's ball during a game of fetch, hold the ball close to your chest, smile at your puppy and wait. As soon as his butt hits the floor, toss the ball. If your puppy jumps up at you and the ball, do not say anything, just wait for the correct behavior. This is part of the learning process. He will be learning that the "jumping up" behavior does NOT get him access to things he wants, but the "butt on the ground" behavior does - a very good life lesson for your puppy to learn. **Tip:** Do not tell your puppy to sit during these lessons; the point of the offered sit is that your puppy is thinking through the process and realizing on his own that sit makes good things happen and jumping up does not.

Down Many people tend to tell their puppies "down" when they want them to get 4 on the floor, then they turn around and say "down" when they want them to lie down. The important thing to think about in this situation is that you have two behaviors; one to get 4 on the floor and one to lie down. That would mean that you need two separate words. For me, "down" means for my dog to lie down. So, if he were to jump up on the sofa and I asked him to "down" he would lie down on the sofa. If on the other hand, he jumped up on the sofa and I asked him to "off" he would get 4 back on the floor.

Level 1
- ❑ Start with your dog in a sitting position.
- ❑ Hold your puppy's treat right at his nose, slowly move your hand straight down toward the floor. ***Be patient!***
- ❑ As soon as your puppy's front elbows hit the ground say "**YES!**" and treat. Repeat 5 times

Level 2
- ❑ Start with your dog in a sitting position.
- ❑ Remove the food lure from your hand and repeat your hand lure from level 1
- ❑ As soon as your puppy's front elbows hit the ground say "**YES!**" and treat (treat was in your opposite hand). Repeat 5 times

Level 3
- ❑ Same set up as level 2, but say your Down cue right before you drop your hand to the floor.
- ❑ As soon as your puppy's front elbows hit the ground say "**YES!**" and treat (treat was in your opposite hand). Repeat 5 times

Level 4
- ❑ Now, on your next trial, say your Down cue, this time only dropping your hand lure halfway down (not all the way to the floor). You are slowly going to lessen your luring to the ground.

Adding Distractions-when you are asking your puppy to work on his down behavior around distractions such as being outside, around guests or other puppies, you must start the training process over at Level 1 and rebuild. Just like you taught him to sit around distractions earlier. He must learn this process just like he was learned it in the living room.

Drop It Playing fetch with your new puppy is a great cooperative game. However, if your puppy does not release the ball, it won't be much fun for you. Drop it is also a good behavior to have if your management slipped and he stole an object he shouldn't have.

Level 1
- ❑ Grab one of your puppy's toys, such as a tug rope.
- ❑ Tell your dog to "Get It" as you wiggle it around so that your dog grabs onto the toy.
- ❑ As your dog has the toy, put a high-ranking treat up to his nose. As soon as your dog drops the toy, say "**YES!**" and treat. Repeat 5 times (if he still has the desire for the game)

Level 2
- ❑ Set up like level 1, this time say your puppy's drop it cue right before placing the treat to his nose. As soon as your dog drops the toy say "**YES!**" and treat. Repeat 5 times (if he still has the desire for the game)

Level 3
- ❑ Set up like level 2, this time say your drop it cue without showing your dog the treat. Wait for your dog to drop the toy, as soon as he does say "**YES!**" and treat. Repeat 5 times (if he still has the desire for the game)
- ❑ If he is not being successful, practice level 2 more.

Drop It Exercise #2

Level 1
- ❑ Have two identical toys, such as tennis balls.
- ❑ Toss a tennis ball about 5' away in a hallway or with your dog on a long leash (20').
- ❑ When your dog comes running back with the ball, wiggle another tennis ball in front of him.
- ❑ As soon as he drops the ball in his mouth, toss the tennis ball from your hand. Repeat 5 times (if he still has the desire for the game)

Level 2
- ❑ Set up like level 1
- ❑ This time when your dog comes running back with the ball, say your drop it word, and wait for your dog to drop the toy. As soon as he drops the ball in his mouth, toss the tennis ball from your hand. Repeat 5 times (if he still has the desire for the game)

Teaching Good Walking Skills

Why I Don't Like Collars Attached To A Leash   Gag, choke, cough, tongue hanging out, eyes bulging, no control.....these are a few things that can happen when leashing your puppy to a regular buckle dog collar, martingale dog collar, choke chain, prong or pinch collar.

As a professional dog behavior consultant, it was pretty easy to teach my dog how to walk politely on a leash with a regular buckle collar. But that does not change the fact that in the learning stages and even around some distractions, my dog may pull at the leash for a moment. And each of those moments of pressure I felt sure were causing damage and pain to my dog's body such as his neck, eyes and spine. For those reasons I began to leash my dog exclusively to a harness and not a collar.

Over the years I started to do some research on the damage a collar can cause and have found a variety of sources that confirm my suspicions of the harm a dog collar can do to a dog and the dog's anatomy. 400 dogs participated in a study on the effects of a collar and leash. 63% of those dogs examined had neck and spinal injuries.[11] According to Peter Dobias, D.V.M, some of these issues can include hypothyroidism, ear issues, eye issues, excessive paw licking, foreleg lameness and neck injuries including whiplash.[12]   A recent study found that intraocular pressure (fluid pressure inside the eye) increased significantly with from the pressure of a collar but not with a harness. Trachea collapse or other trachea damage can also occur due to the pressure around your puppy's throat.[13]

So what kind of options do I prefer? Harnesses and headcollars are my personal preference. I lean toward harness more than headcollars, and more specifically, I like front clipping harness where the leash attaches to a D-ring on the chest. These types of harnesses aid in teaching your puppy how to walk politely on a leash, because when your puppy starts to pull his chest turns around toward you, allowing you to refocus your puppy.

That said, they need to be used as directed to keep your puppy safe. A headcollar that is tight is not safe if you allow your puppy to keep pulling and it keeps his head at an unusual angle. A front-clipping harness that is tight and again pulled to the side is not the correct way to use the tool.

Loose Leash Walking   Every puppy should learn how to walk politely on a leash. But before you set out to tackle this challenging behavior, be prepared to practice *every time* your puppy is leashed and remember to have a lot of patience. This is not a behavior that happens quickly, and it is important to practice walking skills daily if you want to master this behavior. Here are some techniques to use when teaching leash manners.

Follow Me Off Leash (inside the house, or in a fenced in area)   You must create the association that you are the best thing in the world, engaging and exciting. If your puppy realizes how much fun you are, he is much more likely to be attentive to you. While your puppy is close to you and not too distracted, make a high-pitched smooching sound and back away a few steps while you are still smooching. As your puppy follows, praise and encourage him. Allow him to "catch" you and give him a pet, treat, or play with a toy. Repeat this exercise changing direction, skipping and have a good time allowing your puppy to catch you. Remember, this is supposed to be fun for both you and your puppy, so get silly and creative and change directions.

Walking Next To Your Side Off Leash (inside the house, or in a fenced in area) Grab a handful of treats or food kibbles and lure your puppy with a treat to your left or right side. Give him a treat when he gets into position. With your handful of food, place your hand in front of his nose, say, "OK" and take 3 steps forward with your puppy following the treat. After step 3 give him a treat. Repeat this process and vary the number of steps before giving him the food treat.

Walking On Leash Whenever your puppy is attached to his leash, you need to be prepared to work on his leash manners. There is no "off time" when he is attached to his leash. Teaching good leash skills can be very challenging. When you set out to practice leash walking start with a training time in mind, such as 15 minutes. Do not start with a walking destination like "around the block" or you are likely to get very frustrated. If it takes you and your puppy 15 minutes to walk down the end of the driveway, then so be it. You are setting the foundation to a life-long skill of not pulling on the leash. These early stages are vital if you want to have a great walking partner in the future.

Your walk clock starts the time you pull out your puppy's leash. If he is jumping around acting like a silly puppy, just stand there and wait for him to settle down. Once he has settled down, bend down and attach his leash. If he spins out of control and runs off, stand back up and wait for him to come back and wait again for him to settle down. Repeat until you can calmly attach his leash. This may take 5 minutes or more at first, but over time he will learn that running and jumping around will not get you to attach his leash.

Pick either the follow me game or walking next to your side lesson. You can either practice inside the house, outside in your yard, or working toward the neighborhood. Remember your time, not destination. The other option is the treat bag method. This is when you decide how many treats or kibbles you want to give your puppy during his walking exercise. When you are half through his stash, turn around and come back. Because walking outside will be very distracting, you will likely need a high motivator such as cooked meat.

Once his leash is attached, stand very still holding the leash on your hip. Only if the leash is slack will you move. Don't ask him for anything; let him figure it out himself. Be patient, eventually he will slacken the leash. Once he does, tell him how smart he is and start to walk. If the leash gets tight, immediately stop and plant yourself as before. You will probably only get one step at first. Repeat as before, waiting for a loose leash again.

Opposite Direction or Penalty Yards On Leash Another technique is to go the opposite direction when your puppy pulls on the leash. When your puppy pulls on the leash, make a smooching sound and turn the opposite way or just take steps backward until your puppy catches up with you and has a loose leash. Once he has caught up with you, start walking again. You will be teaching your puppy every time he pulls forward, you are not going to allow him to go in that direction.

Become A Statute On Leash I only recommend this technique if your puppy is on a harness. When your puppy's leash is tight, just stop. After you stop, make a smooching sound and as soon as your puppy returns to you praise and continue to walk.

Combinations You can choose a combination of the above methods, even during one walking exercise. The important thing to remember is that you are teaching your puppy that when his leash is tight he will not be moving forward. I will say it again, have patience. Teaching your puppy to walk politely on a leash around so many fun smells and distractions is very challenging and takes lots of practice and experiences, but is absolutely worth it in the end.

Jumping Up

Why do puppies even jump up on people in the first place? Puppies are very social creatures and thrive on human contact. In most cases, it is just because we are taller than they are, and they are trying to get to our faces for a social greeting. This is a pretty normal puppy behavior, but something most humans do not appreciate. Teaching your puppy not to jump on you or your guests takes commitment, follow-through, management and kindness.

In these exercises, you will be teaching your puppy a more acceptable puppy and human greeting routine. Remember you never want to hurt your puppy by hitting him, kneeing him, holding and squeezing his toes or stepping on him. Instead, you will be teaching your puppy how you expect to be greeted and ignore him when he offers the wrong behavior.

Your Family Your first line of defense is your own family. After a long day at work you are probably eager to see your puppy and you may even start baby talking him, "Dexter, I've missed you so much! Oh, you are such a handsome boy!" If you are speaking to your puppy in a high pitched, excited tone you are going to increase his excitement and your puppy will start to become bouncy and jumpy. So, you should tone it down a bit.

Review your exercises in ***Letting your puppy out of his crate pg. 8*** if he is crated when you return. If, on the other hand, he is free roaming the house with the rest of the family proceed by quickly squatting down to your puppy's level and gently rub his chest and talk very softly to him. If he jumps up, stand up and ignore him until he gets all 4 on the floor again. Repeat. It will be a bit of a seesaw exercise for you. Do not yell at him, do not tell him "off," just stand up and ignore him. My rule is I have an "Invisible Dog" when my dog is jumping up on me. Only pay attention to your puppy when all four feet are on the floor, or if he is sitting. **All other behavior = invisible dog (totally ignore).** Once four feet are on the floor, he can receive your praise and attention. If he jumps back up, quickly stand up, cross your hands and look away. As soon as those feet go back down, he "reappears."

Fast Tip You can jump-start your puppy's polite greeting behavior by the use of food or toys. When greeting your puppy, or coming home from work, or letting your puppy out of his crate, have some dog treats or dog food on you or in your pocket. As soon as you see your puppy, drop a kibble at his feet. Drop another piece as soon as he finishes eating the first bite. Do this as you walk around with your puppy, or take your puppy outside to potty. As your puppy gets better at this routine, your kibble drops will be spaced out more. Instead of a kibble drop every second, you can drop every 3 seconds, 5 seconds, 15 seconds, etc. until he no longer needs them.

To use a toy in polite dog greeting behavior you must first find a toy your puppy thinks is very exciting and he wants to eagerly fetch or hold. Sometimes this means having a cupboard full of new puppy toys to keep them interesting and engaging, or you can reserve a special toy just for greeting. As soon as you see your puppy heading toward you to say hello, wiggle the toy and toss for your puppy to fetch. You may need to have a few toys in your hand so when your puppy returns with the first toy, you can toss another new toy for him to fetch. Retrieve the first toy he dropped and repeat this process. Some dogs will hold the toy in their mouths while wiggling around you. If this is the case, you will not need to keep tossing toys. This again is a behavior you can fade over time as your puppy masters the greeting routine.

Interactive Exercise and Attention Please remember that your puppy needs to be adequately exercised every day both physically and mentally. If your puppy does not get quality physical and mental bonding time with you, he is unlikely to be successful. If you are unsure if you provide your puppy with enough exercise and attention, review your ***puppy's log book pg. 55*** Write down your daily activities with your puppy. And when I say "with your puppy" I mean that you are actually paying attention to and bonding with him. Not that your puppy is laying on the floor in the same room. Dog's are Man's/Woman's Best Friends for a reason. They need you and your attention.

Your Guests Mastering polite greeting with your own family members can be quite successful if everyone is playing by the rules. It still will take time and practice, but your puppy should be able to understand the way you want to be greeted. House guests, on the other hand, are in a different ballpark altogether. How you manage this situation will determine your puppy's success. If you do not manage these situations correctly, then you will not have the polite greeter of your dreams.

Management is once again the top priority if you want to have success. If you prevent your puppy from launching himself at your guest, you will then be able to teach him a more appropriate greeting behavior. If, on the other hand, he body slams himself on your guest, he is performing (and probably getting good at it) the exact behavior you do not want him to do. Instead, plan ahead.

Tether, harness and stuffed treat toy When you are expecting guests, put your puppy's harness on and prepare a filled hollow treat toy. Decide which room you and your guests are going to reside in and place a tether around a heavy piece of furniture such as a sofa leg. When the doorbell rings, collect your puppy and attach him to the tether by his harness and provide him with his filled hollow toy.

Go to the door and greet your guests. Take off their coats, say hello and ask them to ignore your puppy. When you walk into the main room where your puppy is chewing on his very delicious stuffed treat toy, sit next to your puppy. Occasionally add a bonus treat while he continues with his chew toy. Once he is finished with his chew toy, attach his leash to his harness, then unclip him from the sofa, but do not leave. Work on some of his behaviors you have been teaching him such as sit, down and watch. Treat him for paying attention and doing these behaviors. What you are doing is teaching him to listen to you, even though there are very distracting guests in the house. Only when he can do these behaviors for you should you go to the next step.

When he is ready and able to focus his attention on you, ask one of your seated guests to reach down toward their shin and wiggle their fingers. As they do that, walk your puppy up to the guests and tell your puppy to say hello. As soon as your puppy sniffs your friend's fingers say "YES!" and quickly move your puppy a foot away and give him a treat. Be careful not to jerk your puppy. What you are doing is rewarding your puppy for politely sniffing the guest's fingers (not jumping up), and giving your puppy distance away from the guest to collect his reward. This will help ensure no jumping. Repeat this process for 5 repetitions. When this is successful, allow your puppy to sniff a little longer before saying yes and removing and treating. This will help him learn to greet with 4 on the floor, but only take baby steps so that your puppy can be successful. Puppies get overly excited very quickly; moving slowly with this training will allow you to keep your puppy's eagerness a bit more manageable, while also teaching him that *guests* are not the golden ticket, *you* are.

When you are done practicing, keep your puppy leashed to you. Only when you start to have a reliable behavior, with no jumping, should your puppy be allowed to run freely with guests. Remember, prevention is the key. It will not do you any good to practice these lessons, then to unleash your puppy for him to start jumping around on your guests. If you do not wish to have him leashed with you, you can use another management tool such as tethering him in sight, baby gated, or put him in his crate. When you start to consider allowing him more roaming freedom, he should respond well to The Name Game.

Inside off leash freedom still requires a proactive role on your part. Once your puppy has proven to be successful over various practice sessions and real life lessons and you feel his Name Game is reliable, you can unleash the hound! But that does not mean a free-for-all for your puppy. Practice randomly calling him to you with his name and rewarding that behavior. You can also have your guests provide food kibbles for your puppy when he offers his butt on the floor routine. Hand one of your guests a fist full of kibbles. Ask your guest to drop a kibble about 2' away from your puppy when he puts his butt on the floor. By having your guest toss the reward away from your puppy, your puppy will move away from your guest, then return to your guest to start the process all over. This allows multiple sessions in a short time. But be careful with this. If your guests do not have good timing, or are overly enthusiastic, or slow it can easily backfire and cause your puppy to start jumping up for the treat because he is impatient. After your guest finishes the hand of kibbles, call your puppy away from your guest. Always feel like you can give things a try but know you can always quickly go into management mode if you are not seeing the success you had hoped for.

People In Public When meeting people in public, your puppy will already be on his harness and leash, which is a great management tool. When a stranger asks to pet your puppy, you always have the option to decline politely. If your puppy is having a hard time focusing on you, or is having a bad day, or you are uncertain about the stranger, you can say, "no, but thank you for asking," as you walk away. You should not feel pressured into a greeting, or even feel like you need to provide a reason for saying no. People really need to learn that not everyone wants to say hello every time. You will actually being doing a service by randomly saying no to people. If someone is approaching you and your puppy and did not ask to say hello first, immediately traffic cop them by placing your hand straight out, palm facing the stranger. You can quickly say, "Not every dog wants to say hello; it is always polite to ask first." Then you can follow up with, "Would you like to say hello to my puppy?"

If you are going to allow your puppy to say hello to someone in public, practice these proactive steps. As the person approaches you and your puppy, squat down with your puppy and slip your hand inside your puppy's harness to guide your puppy to keep his 4 on the floor. It also allows you to touch your puppy and assure that he is happy and comfortable. If at any time he seems uncomfortable, politely move away and thank the person for saying hello. You can also add food rewards by treating your puppy for keeping 4 on the floor. This can speed up the process. Just make sure you are not luring your puppy to interact if he prefers not to. After a short visit, say thank you to the stranger and walk away with your puppy. Be sure to engage your puppy first to help prevent a last minute jump up as you leave.

Your Puppy's Health

Your Puppy's Medical Care Choosing your puppy's medical care giver(s) can be one of the most important things you can do for your puppy. This task can seem daunting with all the veterinarians available. You may have heard some common terms such as traditional, conventional, holistic, alternative or integrative medicine to describe a veterinarian and their practice. These describe the veterinarian's typical approach in the healthy care and treatment of your puppy. But what exactly do all these terms mean?

Traditional and conventional veterinarians make up the majority of practicing veterinarians today. A standard veterinarian with these practices utilizes physical exams, blood work, state of the art diagnostics including MRI machines, ultrasounds and x-rays to name a few. With a diagnosis they treat the patient with surgery, antibiotics or other medications.

Holistic, alternative and integrative veterinarians are not as common in today's market but are becoming more common everyday. Holistic veterinarians also use physical exams, blood work, state of the art diagnostics including MRI machines, ultrasounds and x-rays to name a few. But their treatment plan starts with a holistic approach using chiropractic care, acupuncture, laser treatment, homeopathy, massage, food therapy, herbals, and oils. Holistic veterinarians focus on the whole patient and look to address the underlying cause of the symptom and make every effort to treat the condition with non-evasive techniques.

Both types of practicing veterinarians may use methods from each category, but their philosophy and first line of defense is typically either a conventional or holistic approach.

How to choose your puppy's veterinarian is a personal choice. Ask your friends and family who they take their pets to and what the like and do not like about the veterinarian and the vet hospital. A veterinarian comes with more than just his or her skill set; the hospital layout, location, staff and hours are all things to take into consideration.

Once you have a few recommended veterinarians, call them and schedule tours of the clinics. The staff should be courteous and knowledgeable. The hospital should be clean and spacious enough for clients to sit and wait with their pets with some space in between if needed; you do not want a cramped waiting room where people with stressed or possibly contagious pets are forced to sit close to everyone else. You should have a good vibe when visiting with the staff. When you make a connection with one of the veterinarian hospitals, you can schedule a puppy visit. **Tip:** Keep in mind that your puppy is learning what the vet hospital means, so I encourage you to set up the first visit as a physical examination, not painful vaccinations. If the timing is not right, go into the office with your puppy prior to his scheduled appointment just as a happy socialization exercise where you walk him around, allow the staff to pet and treat him and just hang out in the waiting area. During your puppy's vaccinations, give him treats while he is getting his shots and talk with him.

If at anytime in your relationship with your veterinarian, you feel uncomfortable with a treatment plan or diagnosis, talk to them about it. Tell them your concerns and find out their reasoning behind their choice. Sometimes a veterinarian's treatment choice can be about saving the client money or time, and your treatment choice might be about your puppy's long term health. You are your puppy's advocate and voice, so do not feel intimidated to ask questions or seek a second opinion. If you ever decide that your veterinarian choice does not match your philosophy, you always have the choice to select a different doctor for your puppy.

Vaccinations are given to puppies and dogs to prevent illness and disease such as distemper, hepatitis, parvovirus, and rabies. There are many vaccinations on the market that are not necessary for every dog. Your puppy's vaccinations will depend on your life-style, where you live in the world, exposure to disease, and many other risk factors. You should discuss your vaccine choices with your veterinarian.

Vaccinating your adult dog is not always necessary. Vaccinations come with a high risk and can cause things like thyroid disease, cancer, difficulty breathing and autoimmune disease. Luckily for our dogs, there are blood titers that your veterinarian can perform to determine if your dog still has the immunity required to fight off a potential disease. If your dog's titer is high enough, your veterinarian will not need to vaccinate that year. If you choose to run blood titers, they should be run yearly during your dog's check up.

Yearly physicals from your veterinarian are a must to ensure your dog is healthy and parasite-free. Preventive medical care is just as important as your preventive behavioral care. Your veterinarian will be able to see, feel or hear any signs of disease or aging, and a proactive treatment plan can ensure. Your dog's development is much faster than that of a human, averaging seven years to our one, so as your dog ages, you may want to schedule bi-yearly or quarterly wellness exams. Your dog's veterinarian is likely to request blood work and a urinalysis to monitor your dog's organ function and check their cells for abnormalities. Early detection is always your best line of defense.

Breed health is something every pet owner should consider. A number of breeds are inclined to specific health issues such as heart disease, hip dysplasia, cancer, and epilepsy, to name a few. Knowing what your breed may be prone to allows you to be proactive in his diet and nutrition, exercise, and early detection. For example, if you have a breed that is known to have a high risk of heart disease you can schedule yearly physicals with a board-certified cardiologist. You can also keep your dog fit by daily exercise, keeping an ideal weight, and feeding him a heart-healthy diet.

Health Insurance I am a firm believer in purchasing a health insurance plan for your puppy. Puppyhood is the perfect time to make this purchase. An injury can happen any time without any notice, and can cost thousands of dollars in treatment. Pre-existing conditions can be ruled out if you purchase at an early age and keep your policy current. But not all plans and insurance companies are the same. Each family is different in their needs and each puppy and dog breed varies with their medical care and hereditary and congenital conditions.

When you are considering coverage, take your time in reviewing the different insurance companies, their coverage, limits and monthly costs. Personally, I look to ensure the following are covered in my plan: hereditary and congenital conditions, veterinary exam fees, diagnostic treatments, surgery, medications, imaging, cancer treatments, rehabilitation, alternative and holistic treatments, and specialists. It is always better to be safe than sorry.

Healthy Food and Proper Weight I am sure you have heard the old saying, "You are what you eat." I have no doubt that this holds true for both humans and our canine friends. Choosing the correct food for your puppy can be very confusing, and if you ask five friends and five vets what a healthy dog food contains, you will likely get ten different answers. So let us look at the six main categories of dog food, or dog's diet: dry, freeze-dried, roll, canned, raw and home cooked. Then we will discuss how to read a dog food label, and what kinds of ingredients your puppy needs to thrive.

Dry dog food is by far the most popular category in the pet food industry. There is no doubt that dry food is very convenient and can range in price from cheap to quite expensive. Dry dog foods tend to be high in carbohydrates, which then turn into sugars when digested. Another down side in a dry dog food is that the high temperatures used in the manufacturing process make the food less digestible and nutritious for your dog. This processing takes out almost all the moisture in the food. Moisture in your dog's diet is important to prevent dehydration, kidney disease, organ function, and proper digestion. Adding water to the dry food will not provide your dog with adequate moisture. Dry dog food does not typically help with dental care since a dog tends to gobble up his food instead of chewing.

Dehydrated or freeze-dried dog food is another dog food category that is pretty convenient to give. The manufacturing process uses lower heat than dry, which helps maintain the nutritional value of the dog food. However, once again the moisture is taken out of the product, so if you are using this product make sure you add enough water to fully re-hydrate.

Dog food rolls can either come in a refrigerated variety or one that can stay at room temperature prior to opening. Dog food rolls are less processed and at lower temperatures, which helps preserve the nutritional value. Rolls are also higher in moisture content than dry or dehydrated.

Canned dog food tends to use a lower temperature and is less processed than dry dog food. Again, the lower temperature processing keeps more of its nutritional value. Canned food is also high in moisture.

Raw dog food can come in a prepackaged patty, frozen, or made at home. A prepackaged raw diet is nutritionally balanced with little or no preservatives. Since the diet is raw, it has not been processed and keeps all of the nutrition and moisture of the food unless it is a dehydrated raw. If you provide your own fresh raw diet, you are able to customize the ingredients to meet your dog's needs. You will however need to ensure that the diet is balanced and add vitamins and minerals.

Home cooked dog food is truly a customized diet for your dog's specific needs. This diet will be high in moisture, and nutritional value, will not be processed and will not contain any preservatives. If you choose organic ingredients, you can also ensure that the food is pesticide and chemical free. This diet will also need to be balanced and have added vitamins and minerals.

Reading a dog food label can be confusing and time-consuming, but is truly imperative if you want to provide a high quality, nutritionally rich dog food. Minimally the first 3-5 ingredients listed should be a named meat source such as salmon, turkey, chicken or lamb. The more muscle meat, the better. "Meat," "animal," or "fish" is not a named meat. Meals such as chicken meal are highly processed and may or may not contain skin and bones. Grains such as oats, quinoa (actually a fruit) and brown rice are not bad as some marketers may lead you to believe. However, ideally they will not make up the majority of your ingredients. Fruits and vegetables should make up the other portion of your dog's food.

My personal top 11 ingredients that should NOT be in dog food or treats:

1. **Flavors of any kind, natural or artificial**-No artificial or natural "flavors" of any kind. If it says, "flavor" in the ingredient list, back on the shelf it goes. It is not real food. And if it is not a real food ingredient, it does not have a place in my dog's treat or dog food.

2. **Sugar of any kind including high corn fructose, corn syrup or cane sugar**-Added sugar or high corn fructose is just adding empty calories. Not only are these ingredients bad for your puppy's health, they will also hop him up, and your puppy can become hyperactive.

3. **Sorbitol**-A sugar commonly found in berries, but it is prepared synthetically, so it is now a synthetic ingredient.

4. **By-products or digest**-I can not think of one reason that a by-product or digest would be in a dog treat or dog food. If you are looking to provide healthy food and products for your puppy, something that is left on the floor of some meat manufacturing plant should not make the cut. And these products can even be carcasses from veterinarian practices! That is a pretty scary thought.

5. **Coloring, artificial or natural**-Why would a pet treat manufacturer put dye or coloring in a dog's treat? To please the consumer's eyes, of course. This is not necessary in a food item, especially when the coloring is artificial. Artificial anything is a chemical process and has a long list of possible side effects. "Natural food coloring" is not any better. If the ingredient list does not list specifically what the coloring agent is, then natural can be made by things like bugs and rocks.

6. **Animal fat or anything "animal" or "meat"**-Can you picture the animal when you read "animal" or "meat"? I would venture to say no. If the listing is that vague, it means that anything can be in the bag. A meat should list what kind of meat such as chicken, beef, or lamb.

7. **Chemical Preservatives**-Chemical preservatives of any kind should be avoided. Healthy does not equate to chemicals. No BHT (Butylated Hydroxytoluene), BHA (Butylated Hydroxyanisole), Ethoxyquin, TBHQ (tertiary butylhydroquinone), Propyl Gallate, Propylene Glycol or Sodium Nitrite should be in your puppy's treats or food. BHA, BHT and Ethoxyquin are banned in human foods.

8. **Corn, wheat, or soy**-A lot of dogs are allergic, or have a low tolerance to these ingredients. Excessive soy may contain estrogen that might provide some estrogen-like activity in your dog and contribute to slightly lower thyroid hormone levels.[14] Why risk it?

9. **Glycerin, vegetable glycerin or glycerol**-Glycerin or glycerol can actually be produced as a by-product of diesel fuel. It will be unlikely you will know the difference from reading the ingredient list (although vegetable glycerin is plant based, not from fuel). This is an ingredient in dog treats that helps make a treat soft and sugary. It is not uncommon for dogs to get a big case of diarrhea from eating treats or food with this ingredient.

10. **Binders** such as agar agar, cassie gum (gum Arabic), guar gum, tapioca, gluten, xanthan gum, and carrageenan can block your dog's intestines and even their esophagus while eating. These binders often cause gas and diarrhea. High doses have also been linked to gastrointestinal inflammation and colon cancer.[15]

11. **Added salt, regular or sea salt**-Every living creature needs sodium in their diet, but too much can cause problems such as seizures, diarrhea, and extra water intake. A lot of foods have naturally-occurring sodium, so you do not need extra salt added to treats or dog food. However, salt is a natural preservative, so this alone would not rule out a dog food or treat for me if I could not find a better selection and this is the only not-so-favorable ingredient.

My philosophy is that a dog needs a high meat diet with fresh, whole foods and a lot of moisture. I personally home cook for my dog Dexter, using as many organic ingredients as possible. Home cooking for your puppy does not have to be complicated, but you do need to ensure that you are providing a balanced diet over time and supplementing with the appropriate vitamins and minerals. For more information on how to start a home cooked diet for your puppy, you can purchase *What's For Dinner, Dexter? Cooking For Your Dog Using Chinese Medicine Theory* co-authored with Judy Morgan D.V.M.

A healthy weight is necessary if you want your puppy to have the best chances at a healthy life. Overweight dogs are at risk for diabetes, joint and bone complications, low tolerance to exercise and activity, organ damage including their heart and a higher risk of cancer. Your dog can live longer if he maintains his ideal weight. In an 18-year study, dogs who maintained their ideal weight throughout their lives lived an average of 1.8 years longer than their overweight littermates.[16] Just that statement alone should encourage you to keep your puppy at his ideal weight.

Determining your puppy's ideal weight requires you to do two things. One is to look at your puppy's waistline. Your puppy should have a distinct waistline when looking at him from above, like a little tuck. Second, when you lightly touch your puppy on his ribs you should be able to feel them. If this is the case, you are feeding and exercising him the correct amount. If your puppy's ribs are highly visible, then he needs more calories. On the opposite end, if your puppy does not have a waistline, and you cannot easily feel his ribs, you will need to decrease calorie intake, and increase exercise. You should not drastically decrease your puppy's food intake, instead cut the calories by 5% and speak with your veterinarian on a healthy weight loss program.

You should ideally feed your puppy and adult dog three times a day. Of course, if you are following the guidelines laid out in this booklet, you are feeding your puppy throughout the day during his training lessons, life lessons, and stuffed treat toys. That said, I do recommend your puppy receive about a third of his calories in the morning hours, so schedule some of those training lessons first thing.

Healthy Dog Treats What makes a dog treat healthy? What does that phrase even mean? I am sure a lot of people have a lot of strong opinions on the subject of healthy dog treats. So, I will just give you my thoughts and what I consider when feeding Dexter his dog treats.

Ingredients Yes, the actual ingredient list, not just the photos on the front of the package, which can actually be very deceiving. Even the "flavor" can be deceiving. You might be surprised to learn that sometimes when a dog treat says "chicken flavor" they truly mean chicken flavor, and not any real chicken. The ingredients to avoid listed above are also ingredients to avoid in dog treats. **No**-flavors, salt, sugar, high corn fructose, corn syrup, sorbitol, by-products or digest, coloring, "animal" "meat", chemical preservatives, corn, wheat, soy, glycerin, vegetable glycerin, glycerol or binders.

So what does that leave? Well, a lot of things, really. When looking for a healthy treat you should be looking for real food: things that you can find in real life, not something that is synthetically made, or a by-product of something else. I personally prefer ingredients that are organic, or wild-caught in countries or bodies of water that are known to be clean and environmentally friendly.

Organic foods do not use harmful insecticides, fertilizers, herbicides, fungicides, antibiotics, growth hormones, radiation, or other detrimental ingredients or practices. But you need to be aware of what label actually means.

- **Organic**-If an organic dog treat is labeled "Organic" it only has to be 95% organic. This is where reading the ingredient list is important. Each organic ingredient will have the word 'organic' in front of it if the item is organic.
- **Made with organic ingredients**-Would mean that 70% of the items in the treat are made from organic ingredients.
- **100% Organic**-100% of the items are organic ingredients.

After you look at the actual ingredient list, you should then consider where the ingredients are sourced from. "Made in the USA" only means that the treat was put together in The United States, not that the ingredients IN the treat came from the US. Sometimes you have to do a little digging to find the sources of the ingredients. Most dog treat manufacturers that use only US, or another safe country (there are other countries with better food regulations than the US) for their ingredients will proudly state that either on the bag, or on their website. If you cannot locate this information, I would suggest contacting the manufacture for the details.

Once all this checks out, the next thing you should consider is how you intend to use the new healthy dog treat. Meaning, if you are going to do a lot of puppy training using the treat, you ideally would want it to be pretty much a single source food item (100% cod, beef, etc.). This allows a few things to occur. One, the treat will likely have a high motivational value and keep your puppy's attention on you around various distractions. Two, there will not be "extra stuff" in the treat, so you can actually count the treat (remember, it is really meat) as part of your puppy's daily calories.

If, on the other hand, you are going to use the treat in your treat jar for random snacks, having other ingredients besides or instead of meat would be fine. Just remember, these treats are likely to have more calories and less nutritional value, so you do not want to feed your puppy too many. These should be considered "extra calories" like when you eat a piece of cake.

So there you have it. This is my starting point when determining if a dog treat is truly healthy for my dog Dexter. I do buy healthy and organic dog treats, but I tend to use cooked meat as the majority of my training treats. And those meat treats are incorporated into my dog's daily calories, not just added on in the end.

Safe Dog Chews and Bones

Most puppies and dogs love to chew. Chewing is a very natural and normal canine behavior. Chewing helps alleviate boredom and can even help keep your puppy's teeth pearly white. Puppies and adolescent dogs tend to have a high drive for chewing things. Here we will cover toys and chew items that are in general safe chew items for your puppy.

If you ask ten people what a safe and appropriate chew toy or chew bone is for your puppy, you are likely going to get ten different answers. Over the years, my answer has changed too. I have had new experiences with dogs chewing items, and have learned more information from leading veterinarians on the health and safety of a dog's teeth, and what types of chewing and items can cause serious damage.

My previous go-to for a chew toy was a hard femur bone or antlers. But now that I have been working with some wonderful veterinarians, I have learned that tough bones and antlers easily chip teeth and cause gum damage that is not visible to the eye. You also run the risk of sharp pieces of bone being digested, which can easily cause damage to your puppy's intestinal tract, or can get lodged along the way. By the way, if you look closely at my dog Dexter's teeth, you will see a chipped tooth, from a femur bone. That was the last hard bone Dexter ever had.

Finding the right size of chew toy for your puppy is important too. You want to make sure the chew is not so small that your puppy can place the entire item in his mouth and risk choking, including when the chew gets smaller as your puppy chews it. I would suggest throwing away most end pieces of an edible chew before your puppy can ingest it. The larger a dog toy, the tendency it is to be thicker and tougher, something to consider if you have a puppy who is a hard chewer. But be aware sometimes if the toy or bone is too big your puppy might be able to get his jaw stuck in it. Finding the right chew for your puppy can be a bit of trial and error.

The sourcing of edible dog chews is just as important as the sourcing of edible dog treats. Follow the same guidelines in ***Healthy Dog Treats pg. 43***

Below are some examples of dog chew items that are much softer for your puppy's teeth than traditional hard bones. These will help protect your puppy from chipped teeth or internal damage. Please be aware that not every toy or chew product will be suitable for every puppy. I strongly recommend active supervising when your puppy chews, particularly if it is a new toy or bone or if the chew item is edible.

Hollow Rubber Chew Toys The key to get your puppy to chew on a hollow rubber toy is to stuff it with something edible. A filled rubber dog toy can engage your puppy for a few minutes of chewing all the way up to an hour if frozen. Review ***Stuffing A Hollow Chew Toy pg. 5***

Dehydrated Fish Skins A dehydrated fish skin is a great treat for your puppy that is full of omega-3 fatty acids, typically low in fat and are fully edible. Most puppies love the taste of a dehydrated fish skin and eagerly chew away. A good dehydrated fish skin dog treat the treat will be 100% fish skin and not contain any artificial colors, preservatives or flavors.

Because this is an item that your puppy can eat, I would recommend holding the fish skin while your puppy chews it. This will allow you to supervise closely how your puppy chews the skin, and help to ensure he does not try to gulp it down and choke. It is much easier to remove the skin from your puppy's mouth if you have one end rather than try to run up to your puppy if he is choking and remove it. I now allow my dog Dexter to chew his fish skin until almost the end, then I hold the last bit while he finishes. If you feel uncomfortable, or your puppy tries to gulp the last bite down, you can take the last piece away and cut up into tiny pieces with scissors for training treats.

Bully Sticks Bully sticks are made from the manly part of a bull, and are high in protein, fiber and low in fat. Puppies generally love to chew on bully sticks. What is nice about bully sticks is they start off feeling hard, but are actually soft for a puppy's teeth. Once your puppy starts chewing a bully stick, it gets soft and slowly starts to disappear. I have not seen a standard bully stick break in half. I have seen dog's sometimes pull a piece off like string cheese, in which case I remove that part. Bully sticks are made to be fully digestible, but I do worry about choking hazards. When the bully stick is small enough to fit whole in your puppy's mouth, I highly recommend throwing away. **Tip:** Odor free or low odor is recommended. When a bully stick is not low odor, it sticks to high heavens.

Pig Snouts Are wonderful, soft chew toys. A typical pig snout chew has a soft texture which is excellent for a puppy's teeth, and is high in protein and fully digestible. My suggestion for active supervision holds true with a pig snout. Anything that can be fully eaten by your puppy always carries a choking hazard. It is important to ensure safety with all chew products.

Raw Bones Raw bones are another option for your puppy to chew on. Because the bones are not cooked, they are soft and unlikely to splinter. Cooked bones easily splinter and are very hard on your puppy's teeth. For cleanliness, this is a wonderful time to lay a sheet down and tether your puppy so that he stays on the sheet while eating his bone. Another option would be for him to chew on the bone outside (supervised, of course), or on a tile floor. You can provide the bone to your puppy for about an hour, then either put the bone in the refrigerator for up to four days, or throw it away. Do not allow the bones to get lost around the house or yard, because that is when they are likely to get bacteria build up or dry out and splinter.

Nylon Bones Personally I am a bit on the fence about nylon chew bones for puppies. These products are sold as "non-edible," yet little pieces of the nylon can be ingested (and usually passed), so this poses a dilemma for me. My recommendation for the use of these nylon-type bones is if your puppy is an aggressive chewer and pieces are coming off, I would not recommend the product. Why risk it? On the other hand, if your puppy chews lightly and the bone is pretty much intact, it can be a nice soothing chew for your puppy. If you are going to try a nylon bone, you may need to entice your puppy into chewing it by smudging a little bit of organic peanut butter or almond butter on the bone.

Proper Exercise With safe and proper exercise, you will be able to help your puppy expel some of his puppy energy. However, there are some cautionary measures to take particularly when your puppy is under 18 months of age. During this time, your puppy's body is growing and developing including his joints and growth plates. What this means to you, is that you do not want to overdo your puppy's exercise. Keep exercise sessions, including active play, to under 15 minutes, and low impact. This is not the time to strap him to a bike and go for a long run.

Grooming Your Puppy

Brushing, Bathing, Nail Trims and Dental Care Keeping your puppy's hygiene in tip-top shape is necessary for his overall health. Grooming your puppy is more than just his appearance. Brushing your puppy's coat at least every few days not only keeps it free of debris, but free of mats that can pinch your puppy's skin and cause infections. Bathing your puppy on a regular basis keeps him clean and helps keeps allergens such as grass and dust from accumulating in his fur. Keeping your puppy's nails short helps with his traction and balance. And dental care is probably one of the most missed hygiene regimen in a puppy's care. Periodontal disease is very common in dogs if their teeth have not been cared for.

Brushing your puppy on a regular basis conditions our puppies to enjoy handling and improves the bond we have with them. Caressing our puppies provides emotional and physical benefits for them and us. Most puppies will need to learn this response. Gradual intervals of brushing paired up with treats can help speed this along. Our puppies will learn to enjoy touch only when they have the right experiences with it.

Use your daily brushing time to check your puppy all over. You can place a non-slip bath mat on a table and place your puppy on it, to allow you to access all parts of your puppy with a great view and decrease the pain in your back. Be careful not to allow your puppy to jump off the table, and do not leave your puppy unattended even to turn your back.

Check your puppy's skin, coat and body for any signs of trauma, lumps, bumps or anything unusual. You can use a rubber or bristle brush on a short haired puppy to loosen and remove dead fur. Start at your puppy's head and work your way down to his tail, including feet and underside. A medium-coated puppy with dense fur or an undercoat does well with an undercoat shedding rake and a bristle brush. Long-coated puppies do well with a slicker brush and pin brush. Be careful not to brush too roughly with the slicker brush since it can scratch your dog if used roughly. Pay attention to the areas that easily get matted like under the ears, arms and bottom. When brushing your puppy be gentle and caring. This is not a time to be in a hurry and rip through their coat. If you brush your puppy daily (including under the ears, arms and bottom), you will unlikely have mats to deal with. Make sure you can see down to the skin when brushing, especially on longer coats.

Fuzzy feet accompany some breeds such as the Yorkshire Terrier, Golden Retriever, and Cavalier King Charles Spaniel. If you have a breed that has fuzzy feet it is important to make sure at least the bottoms of their feet are trimmed short. If the bottoms of a dog's feet have fur, that fur can easily mat, causing pain and discomfort, and can even affect your puppy's ability to walk safely. If you choose to allow the top part of your puppy's feet to grow to what is commonly referred to as "slippers," you will need to brush them including between the toes daily to prevent painful matting. The safest way to trim a puppy's feet is with electric dog grooming clippers. If you are at all uncomfortable doing this yourself, make an appointment with a professional dog groomer.

Bathing your puppy is a pretty essential part of any well cared for dog. Not only is it good for your puppy's health, but nobody likes a stinky dog. You should first prep the puppy bathing area. There are a few tools to make giving your puppy a bath much easier on him and you. The first item is a hair catcher for your tub, which will help prevent dog hair from clogging your drain. Second is a non-skid bath mat. If your puppy has a secure place to stand, your bathing will go much smoother. Finally you will want a hand held shower hose with an extra long hose to make wetting your puppy down and rinsing him off much easier.

A variety of dog bathing tools can make the bathing process much easier on both you and your puppy. Non-toxic puppy shampoo and conditioner is a must. A nice dog drying jacket can come in handy if you are going to air dry, or a pet dryer if you are going to hand dry. A few absorbent dog towels and one for yourself would be a good idea. And do not forget the high-value dog treats for rewards.

Non-toxic dog shampoo is very important to me, and I hope it is just as important to you. Pet shampoos can contain many harsh chemicals that may cause serious side effects. Dyes, parabens, alcohol, phosphates, synthetic fragrances, laureth sulfate are just some of the culprits that can cause cancer, skin irritations, and even organ system toxicity. Luckily, pet manufacturers have developed non-toxic and effective dog shampoos. Please visit our website www.perkypawscafe.com for a list of non-toxic shampoos and their reviews.

Before giving your puppy a bath, run a brush through his fur to loosen the hair and remove any tangles. Place a cotton ball inside each ear. You can place an artificial tear gel on your puppy's eyes to help protect them. Remove your puppy's collar and harness.

If you can enlist the help of another family member during your puppy's first few baths, it will be easier for you and your puppy. Use warm water, not cold water. Cold water does not rinse well, not to mention I do not think your puppy would appreciate a cold bath. Start by wetting your puppy's head and work your way down. When you think your puppy is wet, continue wetting more. Make sure you get his feet, face and groin area. This wetting process starts to loosen the dirt and debris. After your puppy is thoroughly wet, shampoo your puppy, but leave his head for last. When rinsing, start at the head to minimize potential shampoo contact with his eyes. Rinse well until all the water runs clear.

After your puppy's bath, you will want to either hand dry him with a dog dryer and absorbent dog towel or let him air dry. Please keep in mind that puppies do get cold. If you choose to air dry him, put a dog drying jacket on to help speed up the process. Once your puppy is fully dry, always brush thoroughly and of course, give your puppy a nice high-value dog treat for his troubles. If you have any problems, or are unsure, visit your local dog groomer or pet salon for help.

Providing you are using a non-toxic pH balanced dog shampoo, you can bathe your puppy as often as needed. Personally I tend to bathe my dog Dexter every 2-3 weeks, depending on his activity and how dirty he gets between baths.

Trimming your puppy's nails is another must. If you can hear your puppy's nails clicking on a hard surface, he is overdue for a nail trim. Your puppy's nails will need to be trimmed typically every 2-3 weeks depending on his diet and what kinds of surfaces he walks on. You will want to invest in a nice quality pet nail clipper so that they are sharp. There are two styles available, the guillotine and scissor style. Personally I prefer the scissor style. If you are uncomfortable about trimming your puppy's nails, take him to a professional dog groomer. If you do it yourself, it is important to teach your puppy to enjoy the nail trimming process, so follow 1-2 below as a handling exercise.

1. With your puppy sitting and relaxed, gently pick up and hold one paw. Hold for a few seconds, praise and give him a treat. Gradually increase the time you hold his paw before

giving him a treat. **Tip:** If your puppy is squirming, you are holding on too long. Try putting peanut butter on the top of your hand so he can lick it as you hold his paw.

2. With your puppy sitting and relaxed, gently pick up your puppy's paw and touch one nail with the clippers. Do not clip the nail. Praise him and give him a treat. Gradually increase the time you are holding your puppy's foot before giving him a treat.
3. You will want to cut just the tip of each nail, before the curve. Make sure you are avoiding the quick which is a vein that runs in the middle of a dog's nail. If you cut your puppy's quick and it bleeds, you can apply styptic powder to stop the bleeding. With your puppy sitting and relaxed, gently pick up your puppy's paw and clip a nail. Praise him and give him a treat. Continue with each nail including dewclaws if your puppy has them.

Dental care should be started as soon as you bring your puppy home. According to The American Veterinary Dental College, periodontal disease is the most common clinical condition occurring in adult dogs, and by three years of age, most dogs have some evidence of periodontal disease. [17] Toxins enter your dog's bloodstream and can affect the kidneys and liver, but a good dental routine can prevent much of this. Your puppy's first line of defense to prevent periodontal disease is you. You can develop a home oral hygiene regimen for your puppy to help combat this disease.

Brushing your puppy's teeth daily with a dog toothbrush or finger pet toothbrush and dog toothpaste is one of the most effective ways to help prevent periodontal disease in your dog. Brushing your puppy's teeth daily helps break up tartar and keep your puppy's teeth pearly white into adulthood. It is important to use a tooth paste specifically designed for dogs. Human toothpaste typically has high foaming action which should not be swallowed. A dog oral cleansing gel can be helpful in keeping bacteria away. If you decide to use an oral cleansing gel, I would advise rotating every other day with actual brushing since this seems to be a much more effective way in preventing periodontal disease.

I have found that most puppies prefer starting their dental care with the finger pet toothbrush over the regular dog toothbrush. It seems to be a little less intrusive, plus you can feel exactly where you are cleaning and the kind of pressure you are using.

Getting started with brushing your puppy's teeth does not have to be a stressful event. Take it slow and introduce the procedure at your puppy's pace.

❑ Squeeze of the dog toothpaste on your finger and slip it into one side of his mouth. No rubbing, no scrubbing. Do the same for the other side. That is it, end of lesson. Practice this each day for three days. When he is easily accepting your finger in his mouth, go to the next step.
❑ Put your finger toothbrush on and a dab of dog toothpaste, and once again slip your finger into both sides of his mouth.
❑ As you both get more comfortable start to increase the scrubbing action inside your puppy's mouth. Gently-do not get too rough or hard. Your goal will be to hit all your puppy's teeth with a little scrub.
❑ That's it! You should be well on your way to helping your puppy have fresh breath, a great smile and healthy teeth and gums.

If you decide you would rather use a dog toothbrush instead of the finger pet toothbrush do the same steps in getting your puppy accustomed to the brush inside his mouth that you did for the finger brush.

Dog chews, bones and chew toys can also be helpful in a good dental program. Your puppy's chewing action on safe and healthy dog chews can assist in removing plaque build-up. You can even squirt a dab of dog toothpaste on the chew before handing to your puppy. Please keep in mind the safety of the chew you are giving your puppy and review section *Safe Dog Chews and Bones pg. 45*

Traveling with Your Puppy

Motion Sickness Motion sickness in puppies is pretty normal. Motion sickness can vary from excessive drooling, panting, whining, restlessness, vomiting, or your puppy being fearful of even entering the car.

Puppies get car sick due to their anatomy. A puppy's ear structure is still immature and not fully developed. This immaturity in your puppy's ear anatomy can contribute to motion sickness. In all dogs (and us humans too), motion affects the vestibular system in the inner ear. The vestibular system contributes to balance and spatial orientation. When this feels out of balance, then it triggers the part of the brain that is in control of vomiting, causing an upset stomach.

Preventing car sickness in puppies is your first line of defense.   The first thing you can do is to acclimate your puppy to his puppy car harness or travel crate without turning the car on. Take your time in these beginning stages so your puppy is comfortable and relaxed in the car harness or crate. This may take a few days or a few weeks depending on your puppy's reaction.

Second step, secure your puppy in his dog harness or crate and start your car. Having a second person would be ideal, so they can focus on tending to the puppy. Open your car windows a couple of inches to help equalize the air pressure inside the car and keep your car on the cool side. **Tip:** If you are using a dog harness, or your puppy can see out the window, you can use car window shades to prevent him from looking out. Looking out the window can cause your puppy to become more nauseated.

Take a ride around the block. You can talk soothingly to your puppy to let him know you are there. Or you can have your helper give him tiny treats. Be careful here, you do not want to feed your puppy too much and chance your puppy vomiting. Assuming your puppy is doing well and not getting sick, you can build the time and distance you travel. Make sure you go on fun outings like the park. Short and sweet puppy adventures are the way to go.

Car Safety When your puppy accompanies you in the car, you should take some safety measures to ensure his safety. Many dog travel restraints on the market do not protect your puppy during a car crash. Most of the products on the market are labeled to stop distracted driving, not to keep dogs safe. Even the products that say "crash test" may or may not have actually passed! Did you know that for most pet products, manufacturers do not have to test their products? Unlike consumer products, there are no standards to ensure product safety. That is a pretty scary thought.

Luckily for us, an independent company has been testing various dog car seats, car harnesses and is working toward testing crates. The Center for Pet Safety is a non-profit organization stepping up to the plate and testing car restraints and working toward legal standards in dog car safety.

At the time of this writing, SleepyPod Clickit Utility Harness was the only dog car restraint that passed their crash test. Upon completion of scientific testing of pet safety harness products that claim "testing," "crash testing," or "crash protection," The Center for Pet Safety has determined that the SleepyPod Clickit Utility harness is the top performing pet safety harness brand of the 2013 Safety Harness Crashworthiness Study.[18] The SleepyPod Clickit Utility harness is priced around $100.

The Center for Pet Safety has not yet studied crate safety, but they are currently working toward that goal. However, Variocage has completed ample testing on their crate safety and published their evidence.[19] The Variocage is priced around $750.

I encourage you to do a little research and visit The Center for Pet Safety's website and look at their findings. As this research becomes more mainstream, it will increase the likelihood that manufacturers will continue to work on the safety aspect and comfortable traveling options for our dogs. www.centerforpetsafety.org

Choosing A Qualified Dog Trainer or Dog Behavior Counselor

Having a qualified dog training coach can assist your puppy rearing. Choosing someone who is qualified, trustworthy, and someone you feel comfortable working with you can sometimes be tricky. In the same way you selected a good veterinarian, you will need to do some research in finding a skilled dog trainer.

Ask friends and family who have a well-behaved dog whom they recommend. Visit various dog trainers' websites and look for their training philosophy, continuing education, and professional years in business. Once you have narrowed down your search to a few trainers, contact them to see if you have a rapport, and see if you can watch a group class in session. During a group class, the dogs and humans should be enjoying their class, look relaxed, and the class should be well organized and, ideally, small.

If you are contacting a professional because you see signs of anxiety or growling, it is especially important to seek out the help of an experienced professional in that behavior. Do not be shy to ask questions regarding their experience with the issue you are trying to address.

A qualified dog trainer will have the following personal attributes:
- ❑ Utilizing positive and scientific based training methods only
- ❑ Years of professional experience, ideally full-time
- ❑ Continuing education in dog behavior; this should be an on-going endeavor
- ❑ Professional and courteous
- ❑ Easy to understand with good communication skills

Becoming a Teenager

Adolescent Dogs Your puppy will become an adolescent around the time his canine teeth start to come in, and this developmental stage lasts until he is about 18 months of age. During this time, your puppy's immature brain is changing and developing, and it can be a difficult and challenging period in both your puppy's life and yours. The best comparison between a puppy adolescent is a human teenager, and, needless to say, this can be one of the toughest times in your relationship. An adolescent dog is more often than not rowdier, mouthier, jumpier, and more obnoxious than at any other time in his life. They tend to have short fuses, test you, and downright ignore you when given the opportunity. The average age of dogs entering shelters is 18 months.[20] So why even bother? Because it is a temporary time in their lives, and they are so worth the effort.

What you can do. Have patience. Have a little more patience. Continue with all your training lessons, play exercises, and prevention life lessons. Focus on all the positive aspects your puppy has already learned and keep up his progress. Have fun when interacting with your puppy. Keep in mind the best way to keep your puppy engaged with you is to be fun and enjoyable, especially during this time. If you have been putting in the work, adolescence will not be as troublesome. If, during your puppy's first 18 months of life, you continue to play a very proactive role in his development and learning, you will be able to have an enjoyable "rest of his life," for hopefully 10+ years.

Your Puppy's Future depends solely on you. When you decided to bring home your new puppy, you took on the great responsibility of his livelihood and his future. Your puppy is a bright being, full of life, who is counting on you to train him and help him develop into a great family dog. You are responsible for his life and well-being. If you choose to work with him only half-heartedly, and do not teach him the life skills he needs to live in your human world, he is more likely to become one of the 4 million pets surrendered to animal shelters each year.[21]

So keep working with your puppy on a daily basis. If you are practicing the exercises in this booklet daily, you are on your way to a well behaved and valued family member. Keep taking your puppy on regular, preferably daily socialization adventures. Get the help of a positive and experienced dog training coach and enroll in group or private classes. As they say, "an ounce of prevention is worth a pound of cure."

And lastly, but certainly not least, enjoy your puppy and have fun!

Daily Puppy Homework Log

Task	Details on progress and who practiced with the puppy.

Taking food and treats gently pg.3 _____

Filled treat toys pg.5 _____

Crate training exercises pg.7 _____

Socialization-New people of various ages pg.11 _____

(at least 5 new people a day)

Socialization-New places _____

Socialization-New things and challenges _____

Socialization-New dogs _____

Handling and restraint pg.16 _____

Relaxation techniques pg.17 _____

Games and play pg.18 _____

(at least 5 times a day)

Preventing thunder phobia pg.20 _____

Preventing resource guarding pg.21 _____

Preventing separation anxiety pg.23 _____

Potty training mistakes & success pg.25 _____

The name game pg.29 _____

Sit and offering the sit pg.31 _____

Down pg.32 _____

Drop it pg.33 _____

Loose leash walking practice pg.34 _____

Going for a walk pg.35 _____

Daily brushing and dental care pg.47 _____

Preventing motion sickness pg.51 _____

Although this list may seem long and daunting, it does not have to be. If you take your puppy to a new park, or new trail at the park, you are likely going to hit more than one category on the list. Practicing lessons such as preventing thunder-phobia, taking food gently, and preventing resource guarding can be as simple and quick as a 5 minute lesson. A prevention program takes far less time and stress compared to dealing with a behavior problem.

Resources

Throughout this booklet I mentioned various products that can assist you in raising a happy, confident puppy. Instead of naming names in print, I have an ongoing list of recommended products, reviews and articles on my Raising Your Pets Naturally with Tonya Wilhelm website. The reasoning is that manufacturers often come and go, and I am always working on finding new products to try and review. To keep updated on the latest innovative products and read dog training articles and tips, please visit my below websites. Thank you.

My Personal Websites

❑ **www.RaisingYourPetsNaturally.com**
- ❖ Dog training articles and tips
- ❖ Dog training videos
- ❖ Holistic dog care information
- ❖ Home cooking for your pets
- ❖ Product reviews
- ❖ Cat behavior articles and tips
- ❖ Pet nutrition
- ❖ Traveling with your dog
- ❖ Purchase my other books direct
- ❖ One on one support and workshops including staff training
- ❖ Dog trainer referral service

Other Resources of Interest

❑ **www.drjudymorgan.com**
- ❖ Judy Morgan D.V.M.'s Facebook page
- ❖ Informative website with regular pet care tips and advice
- ❖ Veterinarian services in New Jersey
- ❖ Offering veterinary phone consultations

❑ **www.tcvm.com-Chi Institute Of Traditional Chinese Veterinarian Medicine**
- ❖ Listing of certified veterinarians offering acupuncture, herbal medicine, food therapy or tui-na

References

1. Blackwell, Emily J., Twells, Caroline, Seawright, Anne, Casey, Rachel A. (2008) *The relationship between training methods and the occurrence of behavior problems, as reported by owners, in a population of domestic dogs* Journal of Veterinary Behavior Clinical Applications and Research Vol 3, No 5 pp. 207–217
2. Bradshaw, John W.S., Blackwell, Emily J., and Casey, Rachel A. (2009) *Dominance in Domestic Dogs—Useful Construct or Bad Habit?* Journal of Veterinary Behavior Clinical Applications and Research Vol 4, No 3 pp.135-14.
3. Wells, D. L. (2002) *The Influence of Auditory Stimulation on the Behaviour of Dogs Housed in a Rescue Shelter* Animal Welfare Vol 11, No 4 pp. 385-393
4. Wagner, S. (2004) *BioAcoustic Research and Development Canine Research Summary*
5. Salman, M.D., Hutchison, J., Ruch-Gallie, R., Kogan, L., New, J.C., Jr.; Kass, P.; Scarlett, J. (2000) *Behavioral Reasons for Relinquishment of Dogs and Cats to 12 Shelters* Journal of Applied Animal Welfare Science Vol 3, No 2 pp. 93-106
6. *American Veterinary Society of Animal Behavior Puppy Socialization Position Statement* (2008)
7. Dunbar, Ian (2001) *After You Get Your Puppy* pp. 145
8. www.Dogbites.org (2014) *2013 Dog bite fatalities*
9. Rooney, Nicola J., Bradshaw, John W. S., Robinson, Ian H. Robinson (2002) *An experimental study of the effects of play upon the dog-human relationship* Applied Animal Behaviour Science Vol 75, No 2 pp. 161–176
10. Simpson, Barbara S. Ph.D., DVM, Diplomate ACVB (2000) *Canine Separation Anxiety*
11. Hallgren, Anders (1992) *Spinal problems in dogs* Animal Behaviour Consultants Newsletter V.9 No 2
12. Dobias, Peter DVM (2012) *Chock, prong and shock collars can irreversibly damage your dog*
13. Pauli, Amy M., Bentley, Ellison, Diehl, Kathryn A., and Miller, Paul E. Miller (*2006*) *Effects of the Application of Neck Pressure by a Collar or Harness on Intraocular Pressure in Dogs* Journal of the American Animal Hospital Association Vol 42, No 3 pp. 207-211
14. Wakshlag, Joseph J. DVM (2014) *Can dogs eat soy?*
15. International Agency for Research on Cancer (1998)
16. *Effects of diet restriction on life span and age-related changes in dogs* (2002) Journal of the American Veterinary Medical Association Vol 220, No 9 pp. 1315-1320
17. The American Veterinary Dental College
18. The Center For Pet Safety (2013) *2013 Safety Harness Crashworthiness*
19. MIM Safe Variocage Test Standard (2012)
20. American Pet Products Association's National Pet Owners Survey (2011-2012)
21. National Council on Pet Population Study and Policy (1994-1997) *The shelter statistics survey*

73669442R00037

Made in the USA
Columbia, SC
05 September 2019

GERMS A

AGRESSION wish you were SCARED B

ANTHRAX NOT! C

MISFITS D

MERRY Christmas

SANTA IS AN ANAGRAM FOR SATAN!

1940 LAKEWOOD BLVD. • LONG BEACH, CA 90815 • U.S.A.

ZED RECORDS

Photo: Bryce Kanights

Still *Rollin'* and *Rockin'*

POSTERS T-SHIRTS & BUTTONS

1983 Out of School Tour (Picture of Reagan w/target on head)($9.00)
1984 JFA Tour T-Shirt, Untitled ($9.00)
1984 MIGHTY SPHINCTER T-Shirt (2 color)($9.00)
1984 JFA Tour Poster (3.00)
1985 JFA Skate Tour T-Shirt (4 color)($9.00)
1985 JFA Paisley Skateboard T-Shirt (4 color)($9.00)
1986 NEW JFA Tour Poster ($3.00)
1986 NEW JFA '86 My Movie Tour T-Shirt ($9.00)
1986 NEW MIGHTY SPHINCTER T-Shirt ($9.00)
1986 RELICS Surfer T-Shirt ($9.00)
1986 RELICS Skater T-Shirt ($9.00)
1986 RELICS Roller T-Shirt ($9.00)
1987 NEW JFA Paisley Skate Logo TIE-DIE ($12.00)
1987 NEW TIE-DIE ($10.00)
1987 NEW JFA Longsleeve Paisley Sweatshirt ($15.00)
1986 JFA Button ($1.00)

PLACEBO RELICS

JFA
Jodie Foster's Army

'85 Skate Tour Skeleton

JFA
JFA Paisley Logo

PLACEBO RELICS

JFA SKATEBOARDS

JFA Standard
  a. 11" x 32" $44.95
  b. 10½" x 30½" $44.95
  c. 10" x 30" $44.95
NEW Don Lincoln
  d. 10½" x 31" $44.95
  e. 10½" x 29½" $44.95
    (Add $5.00 Shipping)
   (Free T-Shirt & Sticker)

JFA RECORDS

Blatant Localism, EP $3.00
Valley of the Yakes, LP..... $7.00
Untitled, LP $7.00
Mad Garden, EP........... $5.00
JFA Live, LP................ $7.00
My Movie, Single $3.00

JFA CASSETTES

Blatant Localism/
 Valley of the Yakes $7.00
Untitled/Mad Garden $7.00
JFA Live Cassette $7.00

JFA STICKERS

Blatant Localism .... $.50
Untitled .... $.50
Mad Garden .... $.50
JFA Logo
 Red, Blue, Purple, Green .. $1.00
JFA Paisley (Vinyl) $1.00
JFA My Movie $1.00

"MY MOVIE"

New 3 song single $3.00

VIDEO

JFA Live at CBGB's
VHS Only, 40 minutes
$29.95 - $2.00 Shipping

Add $1.00 Shipping Per LP or T-Shirt

PLACEBO PRODUCTS ● P.O. Box 23316 ● Phx., AZ 85063

Send $1.00 For Catalog & Stickers